A BUMPY RIDE

A History of Stagecoaching in Colorado

By Marril Lee Burke

Northern Plains Public Library
Ault Colorado

WESTERN REFLECTIONS PUBLISHING COMPANY®
Lake City, CO

© 2007 Marril Lee Burke
All rights reserved in whole or in part.

ISBN-13: 978-1-932738-30-8
ISBN-10: 1-932738-30-4

First Edition
Printed in the United States of America

Cover and text design by Laurie Goralka Design
Cover illustration from *Harper's New Monthly Magazine*, February 1880.

Western Reflections Publishing Company®
P.O. Box 1149
951 N. Highway 149
Lake City, CO 81235
www.westernreflectionspub.com

❦ DEDICATION ❧

I dedicate this book to my fifteen grandchildren, who inspire me every day to keep learning. It is my hope that they will study Colorado history with enthusiasm and learn all they can about this wonderful state.

Whitney J. and Emily L. Adams, Montrose, CO
Ethan Burke, Colorado Springs, CO
Adam, Grant, and Amy Burke, Arvada, CO
Brandon and Walter T. Burke, Wylie, TX
Aaron and Nicole Burke, Colorado Springs, CO
Katie and Blair Stephenson, Castle Rock, CO
Forest, Jane and Sean at Park City, Utah

CONTENTS

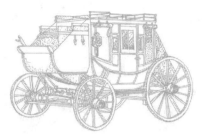

INTRODUCTION

Have you ever taken a four-wheel drive jeep ride over one of the more rough and tumble roads in Colorado? If so, perhaps you can imagine some of the hardships endured by stagecoach travelers in the 1800s. Today, most people's knowledge of stagecoach travel is garnered from watching John Wayne movies, television westerns, and the like. And yet, for better or for worse, stagecoaching has been greatly glamorized and romanticized by the people working in Hollywood.

For most people, images of stagecoaches in the Old West bring to mind thoughts of hold-ups by gangs of masked hombres hovering behind trees and rocks waiting for just the right moment to rush out in front of the coach, a six-shooter in each hand and kerchiefs covering their faces. "Throw down the box, driver!" they yell, along with "You folks put all your valuables in this here hat. You, too, Miss!"

We can only imagine what it was really like in those days, to travel hundreds of miles in a swaying stagecoach with hard, wooden benches for seats, often having only a mere fifteen inches of space to yourself. Stage passengers often encountered rainstorms, wind, thunder and lightning, mud, snow, and rockslides, all with only a thin piece of canvas to protect them from the inclement weather.

Since there is no one alive today who experienced these hardships first-hand, most of the research for this book consists of bits and pieces of stories from pioneers who thoughtfully recorded their stagecoaching experiences in old journals and diaries that were later passed down from one generation to another.

In most libraries across Colorado one can find volumes of books about railroading, wagon trains, mining, dance hall girls, and notable characters of the Old West. People who founded cities and towns, built toll roads, and struck it rich—and entrepreneurs who started businesses, freight lines, hardware stores, saloons, and hotels—have also been written about liberally. But only on rare occasions will the reader find true stories regarding the early mode of transportation that "civilized" folks often depended upon in order to journey out west in the days before the construction of the railroad.

My interest in stagecoaching began at Blue Mesa, in Gunnison County, Colorado, where our family owned property in the 1970s and 1980s. Winding through the ranch was a very old wagon road, still visible in many places today. Old time ranchers in the area claimed that it was an old "stagecoach trail." This sparked my interest, and, after a great deal of research, I found that, in fact, it really was a stagecoach trail and toll road built in the 1870s by the notable Otto Mears.

The newspaper quotes at the end of each chapter are from actual articles collected from various old newspapers of the era.

If you love Colorado history, read on and enjoy these much-neglected tales of Colorado stagecoaching.

Marril Lee Burke
Montrose, Colorado

CHAPTER ONE

THE EARLY STAGES

Restless young men stood about in droves; there was anticipation of adventurous prospects in the air. In the Gold Fields, life was either slump or boom—either way, stages were packed both coming and going.

In the 1800s, stagecoaches were a new and exciting way to travel. The stagecoach had already been used for hundreds of years in Europe, and later it became a popular way to travel long distances in the eastern United States. Before long, hardly a town or mining camp could be found where stagecoach wheels had not left their tracks. It was therefore logical that the stagecoach became a popular way to travel in and to Colorado after the Colorado gold fields were discovered in 1859.

Stagecoaches not only carried passengers but also mail and express freight (articles that needed to arrive quickly). When railroads were built in the East, stagecoach travel began to wane—but this mode of transportation was just beginning in the West. Some eastern stagecoach line owners, facing a decline in their business, saw the opportunity to go out West and begin anew. There was very little public transportation west of St. Louis in those days, so the stageline companies began moving into those regions and gathering coaches, horses, and mules.

Each company incorporated various advertising strategies to inform the public of their services. For example, some companies emphasized the speed of their coaches, which could travel as far as 2,500 miles in just 70 days. Finally, it occurred to the companies that advertising was not

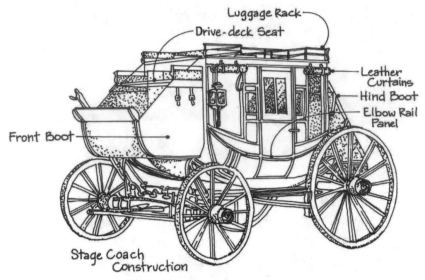

A pen and ink sketch of the typical stagecoach construction.

Sketch by Steven M. Burke

enough; if their business ventures were to be successful, passengers and livestock would require well-maintained roads and frequent stops.

The stagecoach of the 1800s was not the worn-out vehicle often seen in parades and museums, but, instead, a thing of beauty. In his book, *The Overland Stage to Colorado, 1876,* Frank A. Root described his impression of the stagecoach and the lasting affect it had on people who were fortunate in witnessing its glory days firsthand.

> *No one on the plains who was familiar with the Concord coach in overland staging days will ever forget the old vehicle. The stagecoach was a thing of beauty, admired by all, for it took the place of railroads in overland transportation. A vast army of oxen drivers were the most numerous and apparently among the most anxious fellows on the road to greet the old coach. When it approached they would often halt for a few seconds and glance at the vehicle as it came along, quickly rolled by, steadily grew smaller, and in a few minutes was beyond their vision.*
>
> *As the stage whirled on past a long train of wagons, it seemed to be a favorite pastime for each oxen driver to crack his whip as a sort of parting salute for something he greatly revered. Every day these fellows saw a stage bound east and west. They fairly worshipped it, for they knew the stage could cover almost as*

many miles in a day as the slow, patient oxen could cover in a week.

The officers and soldiers at Fort Kearney eagerly watched for the coming and going of the stagecoach. When not on duty, they were almost always nearby when the stage rolled in. It was to them, as it was to all others, the swift-moving vehicle that carried passengers, mail and express. It was important to all travelers and residents on the plains, for three times a week it left mail and express at the few post offices and ranches along the way.

In the early days of Colorado, during the late 1850s to the 1870s, no place in the country outdid Denver as a prosperous staging center. An assortment of routes radiated outward from Denver in every direction. Every day, four-horse and six-horse coaches left for and arrived in Denver from places like Leavenworth, Atchison, Salt Lake, and Placerville, California. Daily lines also left for Central City, Georgetown, Colorado City, and Pueblo. When the gold and silver rush was on, the stagelines also carried mail, freight, and passengers to Breckenridge, Como, and many smaller mining towns in-between.

In the popular *Colorado Magazine*, an article written by Albert B. Sanford entitled, "Mountain Staging in Colorado," told of the first stagecoach that came to Colorado.

Six hundred and eighty seven miles from Leavenworth to Denver and we made it in just nineteen days." This was the announcement of the driver of the first regular stage and express coach to arrive in the Cherry Creek settlement on the afternoon of May 7, 1859. From that day until the Rio Grande railroad was completed over Marshall Pass in the mid-1880s, stagecoaches were operated to a considerable extent in Colorado.

What many considered the best stagecoach, the Concord, was designed and built in Concord, New Hampshire, in the early 1800s. Lewis Downing and his young helper and partner, Stephen Abbot, built these stagecoaches to be lighter than typical models and they rested on stronger wheels. This cutting-edge design gave their coaches, soon referred to as "Concord coaches," a great deal of notoriety throughout the country. Concord coaches were so popular that it wasn't long before every stage driver in the United States and surrounding territories wanted to drive one.

Regardless of whether it was the finest pedigree of stagecoach or the lowliest mudwagon, each and every vehicle that came out of Abbot-Downing's shops was built with great care so that it was able to withstand even the most difficult of terrain and weather conditions. The bodies of each of the various coaches certainly varied in weight, cost, size, and elegance; but the running gear was always built the same, regardless of model. It was the safest and most dependable coach produced in that era, having been designed and constructed using the best methods and materials of the day.

Interestingly enough, the outside of the coach was utilized to the fullest extent possible. The driver and either an express messenger or a guard used the two seats on the upper front of the coach. The top of the coach had a railing around its perimeter, and as many as four passengers could occupy that space. For storage, there was the "boot," which was fastened to the front of the coach underneath the driver's seat. In the back of the coach was a platform where luggage and freight could also be stored. This platform was covered with a leather apron and attached to it were straps and buckles to ensure that the device remained closed during a bumpy journey.

"Thorough braces" were leather straps made of thick steer hide that suspended the coach, allowing it to rock back and forth and side to side. The thorough braces performed better than any steel spring ever could have. Without them, the stage, carrying its big load and maintaining high speeds, would have been fatal to the teams of horses that pulled them, because the

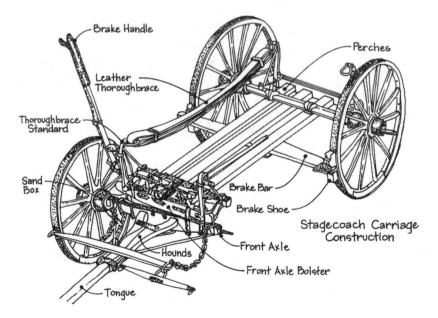

A more detailed description of the stagecoach carriage construction.
Sketch by Steven M. Burke

main function of the thorough braces was to act as shock absorbers for the benefit of the animals.

Some larger coaches had three upholstered benches inside; each meant to hold at least three passengers. This necessitated that a new code of manners be implemented for travelers. One concession for the cramped quarters was called "dovetailing." Since there was not enough room for passengers in the center and passengers on the end seats to all extend their legs out in front of them at the same time, a compromise was reached whereby one leg of each of the persons facing each other would pass between the legs of the person sitting opposite him. Easy enough for men, but for Victorian women dressed in crinolines and petticoats, dovetailing was considered a quasi-erotic experience.

An unknown author penned the following poem after his experience on a stagecoach:

> *Creeping through the valley, crawling o'er the hill,*
> *Splashing through the branches, rumbling o'er the mill;*
> *Putting nervous gentlemen in a towering rage.*
>
> *What is so provoking as riding in a stage?*
> *Spinsters fair and forty, maids in youthful charms,*
> *Suddenly are cast into their neighbor's arms;*
> *Children shoot like squirrels darting through a cage-*
> *Isn't it delightful, riding in a stage?*
>
> *Feet are interlacing, heads severely bumped,*
> *Friend and foe together get their noses thumped;*
> *Dresses act as carpets – listen to the sage:*
> *"Life is but a journey taken in a stage."*

The Concord stages weighed about 2,500 pounds and sold for about $1,200. This was a considerable sum of money at that time. However, the wonderful Concord coach was not the only coach made by the Abbot-Downing Company. They also built two less expensive versions called a "hack" (also referred to as a "mud wagon") and the "celerity" (a word that connotes speed). These were used in place of Concords when the roads were especially muddy. The Concord was a heavy vehicle, and as such was unable to operate in certain climatic conditions that the mud wagons would have little or no difficulty in traversing. Since they were not nearly as fancy as the Concord stages, the mud wagons were built with very little in the way of extras. Instead of windows that closed, they were outfitted

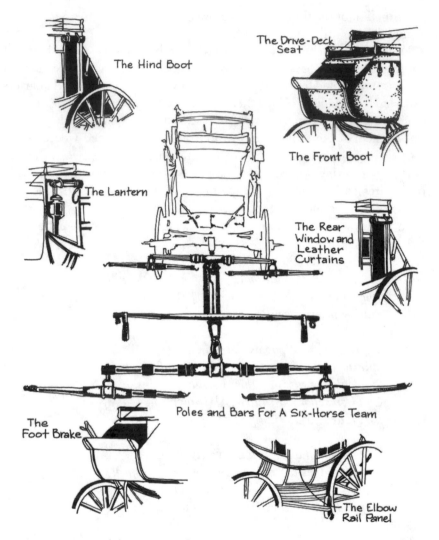

The Hind Boot

The Drive-Deck Seat

The Front Boot

The Lantern

The Rear Window and Leather Curtains

Poles and Bars For A Six-Horse Team

The Foot Brake

The Elbow Rail Panel

Important parts of the stagecoach construction.

Sketch by Steven M. Burke

with canvas curtains that could be rolled up or down, depending on the weather conditions.

There was undoubtedly more mud wagons out west than the deluxe model of Concords. In the early staging days, many smaller stage companies could not afford to buy the high-priced Concord; instead they bought the cheaper mud wagons for about $500. Like the Concord, the mud wagons incorporated leather thorough braces, but the ride was not quite as smooth. The box-shaped body of the mud wagon was placed on rounded irons, which were shaped like the rounded underside of the Concord. These irons rested on the thorough braces, allowing only a modicum of comfort for teams and passengers alike.

Although a few other companies built coaches, none of them could meet the quality standards or the demand of the Concord Stage.

In Robert L. Brown's book, *Empire of Silver,* he described the use of the stagecoach in Colorado's San Juan Mountains.

> *Because of its unique suspension system, the Concord coach was preferred over all other for mountain travel. The body, suspended on leather straps, could swing from side to side without touching the frame.*
>
> *Usually drawn by two or three pairs of horses or mules, the coaches reached speeds between four and five miles an hour. Some rough mountain roads were so steep that the drivers would tie a big log on the back of the coach to help serve as brakes.*
>
> *San Juan staging often necessitated the addition of another pair of animals and the miles traveled in any specified length of time had to be revised downward on many of the routes. In the winter, the wheels were exchanged for runners to bring the coach across the deep Colorado snow.*

Many prospectors, after months, even years, of digging for gold, decided that prospecting wasn't the prosperous life they had expected. Some of the discouraged miners had been wheelwrights, blacksmiths, and wagon and coach makers in the east, so they began ordering fine eastern woods and wagon parts for new factories and shops in Colorado. Usually, they ordered eastern wood because it was hard wood and was, therefore, more durable for building wagons and wheels.

The industry of stagecoach building started taking on a life of its own throughout the West, ensuring that the services of blacksmiths and wheelwrights were in constant demand. There were extensive carriage making shops in Sacramento and Stockton, California. The carriage shops in Seattle, Portland, and Tacoma stayed busy repairing stagecoaches that gradually fell apart while running on corduroy roads in Washington and Oregon. Nearly every western town of any size had a blacksmith and wagon builder by 1865.

Rocky Mountain News, *August 19, 1885*

Two of the long awaited Concord coaches ordered by St. Elmo and Aspen Stage Company owned by Mr. John Stephenson, arrived yesterday in Denver and left on the Aspen Express of the Denver, South Park, and Pacific at 7:15 last night. They are the perfection of stages, have comfortable accommodations for eleven passengers. Nine inside and two outside, along with a good stack of baggage. While very strong and solid in their construction, the ride is easy and comfortable.

CHAPTER TWO

EMPLOYEES OF THE STAGELINE

❧ THE STAGECOACH DRIVER ❧

Stagecoaches were a wonderful and welcome sight when they pulled into their stations, but it was usually the stagecoach drivers whom everyone loved and were most happy to see. Throughout the country where they traveled, stagecoach drivers were the most revered and best-liked men in the land. They were known as a breed unto themselves, and an early author described them to be, "As brave as a lion and as tenderhearted as a woman." The ruggedness and profanity of a driver were rivaled only by his kindness to others and his skill as a reinsman.

One such man was Billy Updike, who most considered to be head and shoulders above his associates, and who commanded most other drivers' genuine respect. A native of New York, Updike was a stagecoach driver for most of his life. In 1860, he was driving the stage in and out of Denver City and Central City for the Western Stage Company. By 1866 he worked for Wells Fargo and Company and drove the "fast line" with Jake Hawk between Denver and Georgetown.

Billy's favorite team was known as the Mountain Maids. Of the six horses, five were bays. They were considered to be the fastest, strongest, most spirited and well-trained horses ever to be put into a harness.

A story circulated among stage drivers in 1868 that Billy drove Generals Grant, Sherman, and Dent from the top of Guy Hill in Golden Gate Canyon to Golden in thirty-six minutes — a distance of nine miles. The Generals were not known to have made any comments regarding their swift journey — perhaps they were simply rendered speechless.

When a driver arrived at a home station, he would wolf down a meal, and then perhaps rest if he had some time before the incoming stage had to be driven back over his route. Regardless, the driver would be ready to take over the reins if necessary whenever the stage arrived.

Passengers riding on the seat beside the driver would often treat him to drinks and fine cigars in order to make the trip a little more pleasant. Drinks were usually free to drivers at the stations, but drivers seldom drank on the road and many of them never drank at all.

On some of the larger stagelines, the drivers' clothing was of top quality and made to order. They were often tipped by appreciative passengers, who not only gave them money, but fine cigars and silver cigar cases, fancy handkerchiefs, sturdy boots, and western hats as well. The drivers were the authority on the road, and their orders were generally followed.

A good driver was always an experienced reinsman. He knew his horses, and they knew him. He knew their limitations and what he could allow them to get away with. He would often call them by name and considered them to be his friends. With the reins placed between the driver's fingers, he controlled his horses with gentle, but complete control. The reins, known as "ribbons," were the driver's way of communicating with the team. Typically, the left hand held three pairs of reins, while the right hand controlled the friction brake — and the whip, if necessary.

Mark Twain dramatized the stagecoach driver in his book, *Roughing It*. He explained that the whip was the driver's most prized possession. It was usually nine feet long, made of rawhide, and almost always decorated with silver in some manner. The whip was, however, mostly used for show rather than for any practical purpose.

Stage drivers were bold men whose duty it was to get the stagecoach across the prairie and the mountains on time. Drivers were required by law to take the oath of mail contractors and carriers, since they often transported mail and express.

Drivers came in various sizes and shapes. Most were in their mid-forties or younger. They were known to be especially polite if there were ladies on board, even though they were generally regarded as some of the roughest men in the country. Often times, though, the driver would break out from a long bouts of silence in order to visit with the passengers and enjoy a bit of good cheer.

Most drivers would know every little twist and turn on his route. He could generally find his way along the road with ease, even when it got very dark. The older drivers, having job seniority, earned the better routes and

Three teams of horses pull a stagecoach on a dirt road near Nederland in Boulder County, Colorado. Driver John T. Carmack ran a stagecoach service from Boulder for several years until about 1914, when Stanley Steamer automobile stages became the more popular means of transportation. A log cabin is in the background. A tree branch lies on the dirt ground in the foreground.
1889 Courtesy of Denver Public Library, Western History Collection

took a few privileges with swearing, smoking, and drinking. A stage driver's route was usually about sixty miles long, and often times it had to be driven both ways. He would sleep or get a long break at the designated station marking the end of each route; but, if another driver didn't show up, he would have to be ready to drive an incoming coach within ten minutes after its arrival. A stagecoach driver was to treat his horses or mules with the utmost care, but not at the expense of running late.

Although frowned upon, the establishment commonly overlooked drinking on the job when circumstances appeared to excuse the offender. In 1865, one driver, in an effort to stay warm, had a little too much to drink. He had arrived at his home station expecting to end his run, but soon found out that there was no one to take the stage on to Denver City. He knew that, by default, he would have to be responsible for driving the stagecoach the rest of the route, but, when the weather turned bitter, he took a few more sips from his whisky flask and was soon very drunk. The wind was still blowing furiously when the stage started down a steep grade, but, by that time, the driver was too far-gone to apply the brake. The coach came dangerously close to the horses, frightening them into a gallop. The passengers yelled for the driver to stop the stage, but they received no answer. One of the passengers climbed out of the window and took the reins. The driver then woke up and insisted that the passenger give them back to him. The passenger, completely fed up with the drunk driver, hit him on the head, knocking him out cold. The brave passenger guided the team and coach into the side of a hill in order to stop their headlong momentum and regain control. While the other passengers looked after the driver, the passenger continued to drive on to the next station. Yet, despite the driver's abysmal performance, the passengers empathized with him and didn't want to see him dismissed from the company for his offense; so they let him drive the last half-mile into the Virginia Dale Station. Some of the passengers did, however, decide to walk from that spot to the station, where a new driver was waiting to take over the reins.

Drivers often had colorful names, such as Whisky Jim, Rattlesnake Pete, Happy Jack, Smiling Tom, One-Eyed Tom, Cross-Eyed Tom, Red Horse, Rowdy Pete, Fish-Creek Bill, and Long Slim.

Frequently, drivers had to deal with difficult passengers. One driver, known as "Mac" McDonough, was a driver on the White Pine to Sargents

John C. White, a stagecoach driver during the mining boom in Eldora in Boulder County, Colorado, poses for a studio bust portrait. Eldora experienced its boom near the end of the 19th century. White drove the stage route between Eldora and Boulder through the Boulder Canyon. He spent the later years of his life living in Nederland. He wears a hat and a three-piece suit with a striped tie.
Courtesy of Denver Public Library, Western History Collection

run in 1883. A single, irate passenger had given Mac a bad time from the time the stage left White Pine. Whenever the coach hit a hole or some kind of rough spot in the road, the man would holler indignantly. When Mac hit an especially bad hole at Cosden — a short distance below White Pine — the passenger yelled to the driver, "For God's sake, have you any worse roads in the state than this?" Mac replied, "Nope, none that I know of." He then headed for a strip of corduroy road with his horses pulling the coach at a dead run. The passenger finally gave up on his protests and simply hung on for dear life. The stage made the run into Sargents (a distance of twelve miles) in a little less than an hour, the passenger having long since been browbeaten into submission.

On the eastern division of the Overland Stage, which embraced that part of the route located between Atchison and Denver City, there were in the early 1860s at least fifty drivers regularly employed — and nearly as many stock tenders. About the same number were employed on the routes between Denver City to Salt Lake and Salt Lake to Placerville, which was the western terminus of the line. The sheer number of drivers alone comprised quite an army of men working on the great stageline. Besides those regularly employed, there were perhaps fifty others who waited at various points on the route, hoping to get a job for a few runs — maybe leading to a position as a regular driver.

There was a man, a college graduate somewhat versed in law, from Massachusetts who had left home to pursue a more exciting lifestyle in the Wild West. He drove coaches on the South Platte between O'Fallon's Bluff and Old Julesburg, and that seemed to be the height of his ambition. He so loved his life on the plains and his new job of driving a spirited four-horse team that he would not even let his family know where he was or what he was doing. He wrote only to tell them that he had abandoned all his academic interests and had gone "on the stage."

Now and then, one would come across a man whose hair and beard were silver from sitting on a box and weathering wintry blasts of frigid air for a third of a century or more. Most were first-class drivers, and among them were several experienced businessmen. Quite a number of them could play a musical instrument. The violin was a particular favorite with most of them. Some had become expert in picking the banjo; some enjoyed the guitar; others blew the clarinet, flute, fife, or piccolo.

One of the old-time drivers was a man named Lew M. Hill, who was an "Overland" driver between Atchison and Denver City. He was employed in the early 1860s on the three eastern divisions of the stageline. In fact, he was a driver and station keeper on the Little Blue and Platte Rivers until the building of the railroad ended the stagecoach era there. Lew first began driving in Iowa when he was young, way back in the early 1850s. In the 1870s and 1880s, he was driving into the mountains of Colorado and was in the employ of Barlow & Sanderson Stage Company, whose lines extended over southern, southwestern, and southeastern Colorado. For some time, he drove between Alamosa and Del Norte, under the shadow of one of the most beautiful mountain ranges on the face of the globe — the Sangre de Christo Range.

For a while, Lew drove the line between Gunnison and Lake City, at the time when those two mining towns were booming. After the gold excitement broke out in Cripple Creek, Lew drove to the new El Dorado, up until the fall of 1894. After the second railroad appeared and took away his livelihood, Lew went back over the range to his home in Gunnison and soon was the head of a stageline running from Gunnison into a new mining camp located to the southwest. Lew was known to be one of the most careful and most respected drivers to be found in the Rockies.

There were many other valuable employees of the stagelines in addition to the drivers. The division agent had considerable authority, being in charge of all company property within his territory. The division boss hired and fired all drivers, stock tenders, blacksmiths, and harness makers; he distributed the supplies along the stageline; supervised the entire operation of the stage in his territory; and maintained the stations.

Next in rank and importance was the "conductor." Many stages had a conductor seated right beside the driver. A conductor's route was the same length as the agent's — 250 miles. He sat on the box with the driver, and, when necessary, rode the whole distance there, both day and night. He had absolute charge of the mail, express matter, passengers, and stagecoach, until he delivered them to the next conductor, being sure to collect a receipt. He had to be a man of intelligence, decision, and considerable executive capability. He was usually a quiet man, who attended closely to his routine.

The position of the express messenger was one of the most responsible positions of all those held by the hundreds of employees working on the stagelines. The messengers were responsible for the safety of valuables being sent back and forth across the country by coach — often a fortune in gold was placed in their charge.

There were many dangers associated with the position of stageline messenger. They often confronted robbers and highwaymen who had somehow learned of the precious cargo being transported. Unfortunately, policing the stage routes was an impossibility because there were simply far too many places where the stage and its load of passengers could be hijacked. Often, messengers took their lives in their hands by riding as many as six days and nights without so much as changing their clothes. The only rest they were able to garner were occasional catnaps as the stage moved across the plains and over the mountain passes. Thus, these men often found it difficult to maintain a crucial mental state of alertness.

The messenger coach had — besides the load of express packages — a strong box so heavy that it often took two men to handle it. It was usually where the most valuable items of the stage's cargo were kept; not uncommonly, it was used to store thousands of dollars in gold dust from the nearby mining camps.

In the 1860s, three messengers were always employed on the line between Atchison and Denver City, as well as between Denver City and Salt Lake City and between Salt Lake City and Placerville, California. One messenger was always traveling east and one west on each division.

Nearly at the bottom of the pyramid of stageline employees were the stock tenders. These rough characters were often fugitives from justice or at least scraped from the bottom of the social barrel. The stock tenders could almost always be seen at the swing stations, which consisted of a one-room cabin of hand-hewn logs, a sod roof, and a dirt floor. They were hired to tend to horses and other animals being kept at their station, and they were expected to have horses and mules ready and waiting within a moment's notice after the stagecoach arrived. They were then given less than ten minutes to change out the horses on the stagecoach with a fresh team.

The stagecoach hunter was responsible for bringing game into the station to feed the passengers and employees. On a hillside located a short distance from the old Virginia Dale Station in eastern Colorado lies a small cemetery containing at least three graves. One grave is that of a certain Mrs. Leach, the wife of the station owner from 1868 to 1875. It is unclear exactly how many graves are there; however, one grave holds the body of Jim Enos, a stagecoach hunter who died during an Indian attack.

On the morning of June 29, 1865, Jim Enos was hunting with the division agent, Robert Spottswood, and Albert Huston. In the early morning hours, Indians attacked the group. The fight lasted all day and on into the evening before the Indians retreated. The fight was a deadly one. Before it was over, Alex Hardy lay dead, and Jim Enos had an arrow protruding from his stomach. He was transported to Cooper Creek Station, where a surgeon tried unsuccessfully to pull the arrow out by hand. When this did not work, he took a pair of blacksmith's tongs and removed the arrow. The instant the arrow was removed, Jim Enos died. The party carried his body back to the cemetery at Virginia Dale for burial.

The Rocky Mountain News, *July 4, 1880*

The well-equipped fast stageline of Robert Spottswood is now running from Como to Breckenridge, over Hoosier Pass to Alma, connecting with Wall & Witter's line for Fairplay and Leadville. Orders for tickets from Como to Breckenridge, or from Como to Alma via Breckenridge will receive prompt attention.

CHAPTER THREE

FAMOUS PASSENGERS

There were undoubtedly many famous passengers on Colorado's stage-coaches in the 1880s, partly because it was the fastest mode of trans-portation in the country at the time but also because famous people had the power and the means to take full advantage of it. However, only a select few of them wrote of their adventures on the stagecoach. One of the most famous of those illustrious passengers who did was Horace Greeley.

Horace Greeley was born in 1811 in Amherst, New Hampshire, and died in 1872. He was a well-known newspaperman and owner of the *New York Tribune*. He was a founding father of the Republican Party, and he often used his newspaper editorials to "reform" the Labor Party and sound his support for homesteads and the western frontier.

Horace Greeley traveled by stagecoach on many occasions, unfor-tunately acquainting himself with some unfavorable experiences associ-ated with this mode of travel. On May 28, 1859, Horace Greeley boarded a coach leaving Leavenworth, Kansas, bound for Denver City. He carried a blanket roll and a travel-worn carpetbag, and he wore a white hat and a linen duster. His trunk was placed in the boot of the coach. On the second day out, he reported sightings of buffalo so numerous "that they darkened the prairie." At the halfway point rest stop, Station 15, they met the east-bound stage, which was a week enroute, as were they. Those passengers turned out to be a disgusted and discouraged lot, having very little good to say about Colorado.

A view of a stagecoach that was owned by Horace Greeley; a buffalo skull is on the roof; sign reads: "Miles Elder's Garage Las Animas Dodge and Plymouth Service, Phone 8." Probably taken between 1910 and 1930
Courtesy of Denver Public Library, Western History Collection

Greeley's coach driver later said, "All the good teamsters urged their mules to the utmost speed the last mile or so approaching a relay station. The mules were trained to go with a full run upon the crack of his whip!" Approaching Station 17 at a dead run, they were descending from the high prairies down a steep, winding road and rounding a sharp bend when suddenly they were confronted by an imposing group of Indians. The mules, terrified, took off in a panic, the driver pulling mightily on the reins in an attempt to bring them under control. When one of the reins broke, the team swerved, and the coach rolled over, bouncing Greeley around inside. The team, now running free, took to the prairie, the driver running behind. Greeley hobbled across Beaver Creek, where the station attendants administered first aid to a deep head cut and a severe leg injury.

Horace Greeley arrived in Denver City on Sunday morning, June 5, 1859, after having been transferred to a faster vehicle about 100 miles out of Denver due to excruciating pain in his wounded leg. He was not transferred to a regular stage, but rather one with fresh horses from the 100-mile ranch.

Greeley eventually made many such trips to Denver City, reporting its flora and fauna in his newspaper. He wrote several books about his traveling adventures, and his observations on Colorado at the time were, for the most part, unfavorable.

CHAPTER 3: FAMOUS PASSENGERS

At one point, he wrote,

> *From the Bijou to Cherry Creek I can say little of this country, save that it is high rolling prairie, deeply cut by several streams, which run north-easterly to join the Platte. We passed it in the night, hurrying on to reach Denver City.*
>
> *This place is likely to be sometime yet before our fashionable American spas and summer resorts for idlers will be located among the Rocky Mountains.*

Little did Greeley know of how grand the state of Colorado would become, and the part it would play in international tourism. Since he was from New York City, life on the western frontier must have seemed pretty crude to him.

☙   ☙

Mark Twain was born Samuel Langhorne Clemens in 1835 in Florida, Missouri, and he died in 1910. Twain rode the Overland Stage from St. Joseph, Missouri, to California in 1861. Eleven years later, Twain described his journey in his book, *Roughing It*. Although his approach is humorous, the book's descriptions are accurate. As Twain notes in his preface, "...there is information in this volume; information concerning an interesting episode in the history of the far west, about which no books have been written by persons who were on the ground in person, and saw the happenings of the time with their own eyes."

The movies create an idyllic impression of riding in a stagecoach: smooth travel in roomy comfort. Twain paints a much different picture: passengers being crammed together with mailbags, jostled by every bump in the road, inhaling dust, and living at the mercy of Mother Nature.

Twain began his journey in St. Joseph, Missouri — the starting point for the Overland Route to Sacramento.

> *The first thing we did on that evening that landed us in St. Joseph was to look up the stagecoach office, and pay a hundred and fifty dollars apiece per person for tickets to Carson City, Nevada.*
>
> *The next morning, bright and early, we took a hasty breakfast and hurried to the stagecoach office. Then an inconvenience presented itself, which we had not properly planned for, namely, that we couldn't make a heavy traveling trunk stand for twenty-five pounds of baggage, because it weighs a good deal more. But*

that was all we could take with us, twenty-five pounds each. We snatched our trunks open and made a selection in a good deal of a hurry. We put our lawful twenty-five pounds in one valise and shipped our trunks back to St. Louis.

It was a sad parting for now we had no swallow-tail coats and white kid gloves to wear at Pawnee receptions in the Rocky Mountains, and no stove-pipe hats or patent-leather boots, nor anything else necessary to make life calm and peaceful.

We took two or three blankets for protection against cold weather in the mountains. In the matter of luxuries, we were modest; we took along but some pipes and five pounds of smoking tobacco. We had two large canteens of water and we also took with us a little bag of silver coins for daily expenses in the way of meals.

By eight o'clock everything was ready, and we were on the other side of the river. We jumped on the stage, the driver cracked his whip, and we rolled away, and left 'the states' behind us....

Our coach was a great swinging and swaying stage, of the most sumptuous description, an imposing cradle on wheels. It was drawn by six handsome horses, and by the side of the driver sat the 'conductor', the legitimate captain of the craft; for it was his business to take charge of the mail, baggage, express matter and passengers.

We changed horses every ten miles, all day long, and fairly flew over the hard, level road. We jumped out and stretched our legs every time the coach stopped, and so the night found us still not tired.

The next day, the stage suffered a breakdown forcing its passengers to evacuate while repairs were made. The conductor lays the blame for the mishap on the extra weight of too many mailbags. After throwing half the mail onto the prairie, the stage resumed its journey.

Whenever the stage stopped to change horses, we would wake up, and try to recollect where we were, and succeed, and in a minute or two the stage would be off again, and we likewise. We began to get into country threaded here and there with small streams. These had high banks on each side, and every time we flew down one bank and scrambled up the other, our party inside got mixed up somewhat. First we would all lie down in a pile at the forward end of the stage, nearly in a sitting position, and in a second we would shoot to the other end and stand on our heads. And we would sprawl and kick, too and ward off ends and corners of mailbags that came lumbering over us and as the dust rose from the tumult, we would all sneeze in chorus, and the majority of us would grumble, and say something hasty like, "Take your elbow out of my ribs."

After supper, a woman got in, who lived about fifty miles further on and we three had to take turns sitting outside with the driver. Apparently she was not a talkative woman. She would sit there in the twilight and fasten her eyes on a mosquito rooting into her arm, and slowly she would raise her other hand till she had his range and then she would launch a slap at him that would have jolted a cow; and after that she would sit and contemplate the corpse with tranquil satisfaction, for she never missed her mosquito; she was a dead shot at short range. I sat by this grim woman and watched her kill thirty or forty mosquitoes and waited for her to say something, but she never did. So I finally opened up the conversation myself. I said, "The mosquitoes are pretty bad, around here, madam." "You bet!" she said.

After we left Julesburg, on the South Platte, I was sitting with the driver when he said, "I can tell you a most laughable thing indeed, if you would like to listen to it. Horace Greeley went over this same road once. When he was leaving he told the driver that he had an engagement to lecture at Placerville and was very anxious to go through quickly. The driver cracked his whip and started off at an awful pace. The coach bounced up and down in such a terrific way that it jolted the buttons of Horace's coat, and finally shot his head clean through the roof of the stage. He yelled at the driver and begged him to go easier and said he wasn't in as much of a hurry as he was a while ago. But the driver said, 'Keep your seat, Horace, and I'll get you there on time,' and you bet he did, too, what was left of him."

🌿 🌿

Edward Bliss was one of the editors of the *Rocky Mountain News* in Denver in 1862. He described his stage trip in the company of General Bela M. Hughes, then president of the stageline.

We left Denver City on the morning of October 18, 1862, in one of the comfortable and luxurious coaches of the Overland Stage Line. The day was bright and beautiful, not a cloud flecked the heavens, and a mild breeze from the mountains furnished the very finest and purest atmosphere for the lungs. We arrived at Boone's Station on Boulder Creek in time for a good dinner, such only as can be obtained where a well-managed and amply supplied dairy furnishes milk, butter and cheese. Mr. Boone has a fine ranch under excellent cultivation. His dairy house is a well-constructed stone building, containing among other conveniences, a mammoth churn driven by waterpower.

Early in the evening we arrived at Laporte, on the Cashe la Poudre River, where we met Captain Allen of the Kansas Sixth, and several of his associate officers. Captain Hardy, of the Second Colorado Volunteers, was encamped a short distance from Captain Allen's command, but the limits of our stay gave us no opportunity to pay our respects to him. A short distance beyond Laporte, the road gradually ascends until the Black Hills are reached. The ride through these hills was a most delightful and exhilarating treat.

At midnight we drew up at Virginia Dale Station, the residence and headquarters of Mr. Jack Slade, one of the division

A stagecoach leaves the Virginia Dale Overland Trail Station in Virginia Dale (Larimer County, Colorado). The station is plastered and has a porch and chimney. A man leads horses into a log stable nearby. Shows men on horseback and chickens near the stable.

A photographic print of a watercolor by William Henry Jackson
Courtesy of Denver Public Library, Western History Collection

agents of the stage line. Nature, with her artistic pencil, has been most extravagant with her drawings. Even in the dim starlight, its beauty was most striking and apparent. The dark evergreens dotted the hillsides and occasionally a giant pine would tower above its dwarf companions, like a sentinel on the outposts of a sleeping encampment.

In Mary Ellen Gilliland's book, *The Summit*, she tells of the wild adventures of authoress Alice Polk-Hill when she traveled by stagecoach from Breckenridge to Frisco in the late 1800s. The high Continental Divide passes provided thrills and spills for stagecoach travelers. But Alice Polk-Hill encountered adventure on a simple stagecoach ride from Breckenridge to Frisco, practically a flatland trip: Her coach went through a flash forest fire. She told the tale in her book, *Colorado Pioneers in Picture and Story*.

> *Now arose the debate whether we should go to Leadville by way of Como or Frisco. We were informed that the coach left for Frisco every morning and the road was level and smooth through the prettiest valley ever seen..*
>
> *Mr. Smith, a walking embodiment of common sense, and the "brake and balance wheel" of the party, gave us advice that Punch gives to people about to be married, "Don't." But he might as well have said, "Do." For we immediately engaged passage on the stage and I began to plan for myself a seat with the driver, for drivers are said to be living, breathing, talking encyclopedias of western lore.*
>
> *Promptly at the appointed hour the horn blew, we gathered our traps and were soon on the veranda of the hotel. When the coach arrived, I bounded to the front seat, eager that my chat with the driver would not prove a delusion. The driver regaled me with stories of lost loves in the San Juans, but suddenly the stories ceased.*
>
> *There was no more time for talking, for we were drawing near a fire in the mountains. The sight was grand; the long red tongues of fire were twining and lapping around the lofty pines up to the very top, and flying off in flags and sheets above.*
>
> *We began to feel the heat as the wind was in our direction. The flames had closed in back of us, cutting off any and all retreat, and onward we must go.*

I hoisted my sun umbrella to keep off the sparks. Vesuvius couldn't hold a candle to them. The whole region round about seemed to be on fire. My umbrella was reduced to a skeleton.

Finally we all curled down in the bottom of the stage, like breakfast bacon in a frying pan, except the driver, for he had to use his energies to keep the frantic horses in the road; as it was they traveled zigzag country. He could occasionally tell us to "keep cool," but it was a difficult thing to do under the circumstances.

We were a sorry looking outfit when we arrived in Frisco. "Oh, My!" and "Duty" were minus mane and tail, and slightly cooked in spots. It was a burning shame.

❦ ❦

Samuel Bowles was a well-known journalist traveling overland by stage-coach with the Vice-President of the United States. Arriving in the middle of the night at a home station, the Vice-President was refused breakfast because he had arrived at such a late hour. However, having had accumulated considerable experience in traveling by stage, Bowles was not surprised when the request was finally granted after the stagecoach driver exclaimed that he, too, was hungry.

Many famous stagecoach passengers traveled through Golden, Colorado, as it was the gateway to the Colorado goldfields. In the summer of 1868, one of the most famous passengers ever to ride a Colorado stage came quietly to Golden in order to escape the turbulence of his presidential campaign. General Ulysses S. Grant, accompanied by his son, U.S. Grant, Jr., along with his friends and fellow generals, William Tecumseh Sherman and Phillip Sheridan, stepped down from the Wells Fargo Stagecoach onto Washington Avenue.

Sherman had talked General Grant into visiting the Colorado Rocky Mountains, and they had invited Sheridan to come along. They stayed in Colorado for a week, wearing civilian clothes the entire time so that they might remain anonymous and unrecognized. However, some locals *did* recognize them as the group rambled around the town. When they traveled on to Georgetown, Wells Fargo & Co. carried the generals free of charge. General Grant was so impressed by the hospitality of the town that he returned in the 1870s after becoming President of the United States. He lodged at the Overland House, dined at the Golden House, and smoked cigars in front of the Loveland Block.

The Gunnison News Champion:

According to Mr. Lewis H. Easterly, the last time he saw General Grant was in July of 1880. "He was driving a mule team down Ohio Creek toward Gunnison. It was a warm summer day and the General was making a tour of mining camps of Gunnison country, shortly before returning from his trip around the world. I had often seen General Grant during Civil War times.

I was walking up the road with Charley Collins, when I saw the mule team approaching and was pretty sure it was General Grant and his party. I saluted, as became a soldier, and Grant stopped and returned the salute and inquired if that was Gunnison where a cloud of dust hung over the lower valley, about seven miles down. There were no trees or grass growing there then.

General Grant and his party stopped in Gunnison, stayed at the Mullin House in west town and made several trips into surrounding territory. One of these was Steuben Creek, which he labeled S.O.B. Creek, because of the bad roads. The name still sticks."

CHAPTER FOUR

HORSES, MULES, AND OXEN

The beautiful old stagecoaches with all of their accoutrements, including the men that drove them, were aptly remembered in American literature; however, we also must not forget the faithful animals that made this fast service possible. Horses, mules, and oxen provided the pulling power for stagecoaches and wagons in the early West. Four- or six-horse teams usually pulled stagecoaches, but occasionally mules were used, depending on the terrain. Most drivers and tenders generally treated their horses and mules with great respect. A contemporary writer of the early 1800s gave a brief but colorful description of early stagecoach drivers and their teams.

> *Every horse had a name. It was "Git up, Joe", or "G'wan boys and gals", or "You are shirky, Bill". "Ben, you want touching up? "If you don't do better, Ben, I'll have to trade ya for a mule." There were all kinds of colorful expressions. Some of the drivers would fret a team to death while others would get over the road and you would hardly hear a word to the team.*

It seems Americans have always longed for faster transportation. In this modern age of spacecraft, racecars that can travel nearly 200 miles per hour, high-speed trains, and jumbo jets, it's hard to imagine stagecoaches as being a fast and efficient method of travel. However in the 1800s, the stagecoaches of the West created quite a stir with their remarkable speed.

Passengers clambered to get a ride on the newest, fastest transportation available.

Fortunes were invested in the finest stagecoaches, stations, horses, and men to give the West the best possible passenger and mail service. One of the more famous stageline owners, Ben Holladay, began with over 2,000 head of horses and mules. When the stations were built along his line, he acquired even more. Horses were high priced at that time because of the huge demand for them resulting from the Civil War. During those years, St. Louis was considered to be the horse-trading capital of the world. Expert buyers, possessing great skill and judgments, purchased some of the best quality horses there for the stage.

When buying stage horses, many things needed to be considered, such as speed, weight, and color coordination for matching teams. Ben Holladay instructed his stock buyers to purchase only the best livestock and to take great care of them.

Although Ben Holladay preferred gray and white teams, the bay and brown animals were usually predominate. It was said that the old dapple-gray's established a record for doing fifteen miles in fifty-five minutes on the road from Denver City to Golden. There were different weight classes of horses for performing different jobs. On the six-horse strings, the team nearest the coach was referred to as "wheel horses" or "wheel mules," and they were the heaviest of the animals. These horses and mules weighed anywhere from one thousand to twelve hundred pounds. In the mountains, wheel horses were often referred to as "tongue-horses."

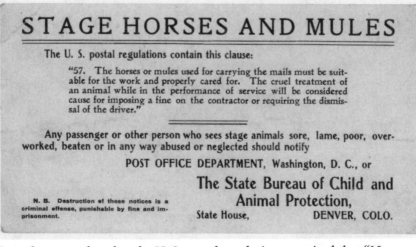

Stage horses and mules: the U. S. postal regulations required that "No animals should be abused"
Courtesy of Denver Public library, Western History Collection

CHAPTER 4: HORSES, MULES AND OXEN

Men on horseback chase a stagecoach during the filming of Robbery of the Leadville Stage *in Bear Creek Canyon (Jefferson County), Colorado.*
Image courtesy Colorado Historical Society CHS-B1683

Buyers needed to also factor in how well the horses had been broken in and whether they would make good "wheelers" or "lead teams." Wheelers and leaders were well-proportioned, well-fed, and well-cared for. Mountain horses and mules had to be of different stock than those needed for the plains. They had to be tough, high-spirited, and exceptionally quick in order to meet the needs of mountain staging.

Stageline owners could not find good drivers who would be willing to work on a poorly outfitted vehicle, so it behooved them to make good choices. If a horse or mule developed soreness, a limp, or certain bad habits, it was retired from service. In particular, stageline companies had to have speedy livestock for outrunning Indian ponies in case of attack. Their theory was that an "expensive live horse" was always better than a slower, albeit cheaper, one riddled with arrows. The owners also wanted a team that could make a grand entrance into each town it passed through by moving at a full gallop. It was good publicity for the company, as the locals were usually thrilled by the breathtaking speed of the stage.

Fast horses were also needed as stagecoach drivers made every possible effort to get the mail to designated stations and towns in a manner that was both prompt and safe. High speeds could be easily attained on the prairie divisions as long as there was no Indian trouble to be encountered. Sometimes, however, power was more helpful than speed when Mother Nature had other ideas. Delays were often the result of heavy rains, which caused knee-deep mud, washouts, and raging streams. In the mountains, snow was the enemy of the stagelines and could often cause delays of several days or more. Some of the wheelers working on the mountain routes were enormous fellows, and a six-horse team would be greatly admired, the animals being all the same shade, and tapering off nicely from the wheelers down to the leaders.

Drivers also wanted fast horses since masked outlaws could throw off a coach's schedule, not to mention relieving it of payrolls and gold shipments. Stage owners could not afford to lose the time it took for the bandits to line up all the passengers and search their purses and baggage — not to mention the bad publicity, injury, or death. If gunfire broke out, a driver or horse would occasionally be killed, further delaying the coach from its intended destination. In spite of all the delays and mishaps, passengers still chose the stagecoach as the safest and fastest mode of travel.

Drivers and stagecoach line owners believed that six-horse teams were more efficient than four-horse teams in terms of both endurance and speed. Four-horse teams were used quite often, but were taxed to their limit with extra-heavy loads. Owners would have used four-horse teams more often, being as how they were more economical, but they knew that it was in their best interest to use six-horse teams when at all possible.

Relay stations kept a small herd of horses available to replace sick or injured stock, and for incoming stages needing fresh horses. When the stage arrived at a station, it was the duty of the stock tender to have the fresh teams harnessed and ready to go. About ten minutes was allotted for the change, but many stock tenders could perform the task in just under five.

While many drivers would sit on the box of the coach while the tenders changed the horses, other drivers would jump down to give the tender a hand. The lead team was unhooked first and then taken away. The swing team was next, followed by the wheelers.

The fresh teams were immediately driven out to take their places. The largest horses were used as wheelers, and the smaller, gentler ones were harnessed in the lead positions. Those horses that were friskier were placed in the middle, making it easier for them to be kept under control.

OFF LEADER
OFF SWING
OFF WHEELER

NEAR LEADER
NEAR SWING
NEAR WHEELER

THE SIX HORSE "HITCH"

The six horse "hitch" shows how the driver had to drive a stagecoach.

Sketch by Steven M. Burke

Each station had to keep large supplies of grain on hand because eating only hay made the horses lose both flesh and spirit, and, before long, they would be unfit for the work required of them. Some stage owners spent huge sums each year on grain and hay. When Indian trouble broke out, soldiers guarded some of the stage stations that had their own hay or grain fields, especially during harvest.

There were many challenges to be faced by stage drivers and their teams on Colorado's mountain roads. It took a skilled driver to maneuver the stage and team over a narrow, winding road. The driver had to turn each pair of animals separately to keep them from becoming entangled with each other and accidentally overturning the stage. It was reported that many passengers preferred riding at night so they didn't have to see the narrow roads and steep cliffs that they had to traverse.

Most drivers were so busy getting their teams around narrow bends and horseshoe-shaped turns that they didn't have time to use their whip. Very skilled drivers only carried them as a symbol of their importance and the potential power they had over the horses.

Company officials, such as division agents and superintendents, frequently traveled their lines to make sure that every animal and its harness was being taken care of properly. Some drivers were very particular about their harness, taking the time to keep them well-oiled and looking almost as good as new.

The stock used on some of the mountain stagelines actually became famous. Billy Updike drove a string of six bays in and out of Denver City for some time. Perhaps the most handsome team was a group of snow-white colored horses that ran first on the Central City line, then into Georgetown, and finally into Leadville. The leaders of this beautiful team were called "Turk" and "Clothesline."

When the South Park road got as far as Morrison, a famous sorrel team was used. The name of one of its leaders was "Old Cap." He was a definite favorite with Billy McClelland, the noted messenger and afterwards stage proprietor, who kept Old Cap for a number of years after quitting the staging business. The old animal's last run was over the shelf road of Mosquito Pass.

Nearly every driver had a decided affection for the horses they had driven a long time. So strong was their love for them that it was often a matter of comment. Some drivers were so devoted to their teams that they cared for them personally in the stable rather than trust a stock tender to do it.

View of a Wells Fargo stage barn in Loveland, Larimer County, Colorado; shows a frame stable with Dutch doors. Photographed by Harold M. Dunning, Loveland, Colorado, in 1925.
Courtesy of Denver Public Library, Western History Collection

CHAPTER 4: HORSES, MULES AND OXEN

In the mountainous regions of Colorado, oxen, mules and horses were often required to meet the need of mining, thereby making the animals quite expensive. It was quickly realized that there was a great wealth to be found in the stagecoaching business. Local ranchers also profited by selling hay and grain for the huge number of animals found in the mountains during the winter months. It was also necessary to build facilities for the animals, such as barns, corrals, and livery stables.

The mortality rate for horses and mules in the Colorado mountains was extremely high, owing to steep inclines and narrow mountain roads. Mules and horses that died in the harness were often disengaged and unceremoniously thrown over the side of a mountain. There was an early Colorado saying that you could find your way over any steep mountain trail just by the strong smell.

Not all animals were "kicked over the side," however. Despite the problems of moving such huge animals, most mining camps buried their horses and mules in animal graveyards for sanitary reasons. In fact, laws were often on the books that required an animal to be buried within twenty-four hours of its death. Ouray had a large animal cemetery across from the American Nettie Mill north of town. The graveyard later became a lovely park and picnic area but, knowing its former use, old time miners were reluctant to linger.

Interestingly, the most used horse for the single rider in the mining regions was the wild bronco. It was not a separate species but, rather, a member of the mustang family. The wild bronco was a small horse so surefooted that it could skillfully pick its way over narrow and winding passes along mountain trails barely a foot wide. The wild bronco was so adept at these dangerous trails that, if he fell down, he could usually get up again without getting off the trail. Because the little wild bronco was so tough and agile, he had great staying power in the mountains of Colorado.

Of all the stagelines, perhaps the Wells Fargo horses were treated with the greatest gentleness and respect. In the property book, the horses' names, colors, and ages were entered at the time of purchase. Their height was measured in "hands," one hand being about four inches. Their weight and height was recorded, and, occasionally, a number was tattooed in their lower lip for identification purposes.

Wells Fargo referred to male animals as "horses." All female animals were called "mares." It seems that horses were used more often than mares, but they both received excellent care. In the morning, the horses were cleaned, and, in the evening, they were rubbed down and had their feet cleaned out before getting fed. They were given four to six quarts of oats per meal and between ten and fifteen pounds of hay every day. They were fed every six hours, day and night, and always had a drink before feeding. On Saturdays, they were fed a bran mash instead of oats at the evening meal.

The Wells Fargo Stagecoach line purchased a variety of items to help meet the needs of their animals. Some of these items can still be found in stables today. Inflation was a problem. A horse collar purchased in 1897 cost about $1.75. In 1899 and 1902, this same collar cost Wells Fargo $2.50 each. Because of the sweat of the hard working animals, the collars only lasted about six or seven years. By 1908, the cost of the same collar was $4.00.

When railroads came to Colorado, the horse populations and the number of stages decreased. Slowly the public perception of the horse became more that of a pleasure animal and less of a workhorse. The horse became a family friend and companion. Many breeds of horses that were at one time nearly extinct have now been revived. The future of horse populations looks promising all around the globe. Finally the horse is getting respect and admiration worldwide for its contribution to the country and the west.

Horses weren't the only animals used for pulling stagecoaches. During the 1800s, mules were in constant demand for coaching and freighting. On the western end of the stagecoach lines, mules were often used instead of horses. Many stageline owners believed that mules had more stamina than horses and could better pull the coaches out of deep sand and bogs. Mules were believed to have more endurance but not more speed. If speed was required, horses were always used. Mules generally had better footing on steep and treacherous trails than horses did. The price for a mule ran as much as two to four hundred dollars in the western region of the United States.

One well-known mule team was called the "Spike Team." It consisted of five dark brown mules nearly all the same size. The two heaviest mules were hitched nearest the coach, then the two lighter mules came next, and, lastly, the lightest of all the mules, hitched by itself in the lead. The Benham mules that comprised the Spike Team were well-known for being able to pull a heavily loaded stagecoach over rocky or sandy roads better than any of the horse teams. This perfectly matched team ran in and out of Denver City, and, at one time, it was even the fastest team on the entire Overland Stage line.

A particular incident concerning mules that was somewhat exciting and, at the same time, not a little amusing, occurred on one of Frank A. Root's journeys west. In the fall of 1863, at Midway Station on the Platte River, a stock tender who had been drinking into the late hours of the night wandered into the stable and staggered into one of the stalls where a span of mules were standing. Quicker than you could say, "Jack Robinson," the long-eared animals lifted him bodily from the ground with their heels, only to have him land next to another span of mules in a stall situated on the opposite side of the stable. Before the poor fellow had time to assess his situation, the mules once more kicked him, landing him back against the heels of the first span. They instantly kicked him again, but this time he landed on the ground at the center of the stable. One of the drivers who was in the barn at the time and witnessed the lively and extraordinary kicking bout, had expected the life to be kicked out of the stock tender, his body reduced to a mass of pulp; but, strange to say, the fellow was barely injured, being too full of liquor to be hurt by a pummeling that would undoubtedly have killed a sober man.

In direct contrast to the fast stage horses and mules, but worth mentioning, are oxen. Oxen did not pull the stagecoaches, but they were very important to freighting as they could pull huge loads — two or three wagons at a time. Oxen hooves were either split or cloven, like that of a cow. Their shoes were curved pieces of metal — one on each side of the hoof. Oxen were cantankerous creatures and did not like to be shod, so, in retaliation, they would lie down and curl their feet under them. However, the big, sturdy animals got good traction on muddy roads and river bottoms, so were almost always used for freighting. Their gait, however, was slow and plodding, rarely exceeding two miles an hour.

This photo of an oxen shoe found on the old stagecoach trail on Blue Mesa, Gunnison County.

Photo by Author

The Gunnison Review, *September 11, 1880*

If you would like to take a safe and speedy journey from Gunnison east, take J. L. Sanderson's Stageline. It is a ride of twelve hours by daylight over Otto Mears' Toll Road, via Marshall Pass. The Marshall Pass Toll Road is perhaps the finest road in Colorado. One of the most careful and experienced drivers in the state holds the ribbons and takes you over this rugged scenery of Marshall Pass with six horses, making time at the rate of nearly ten miles an hour on the eastern slope.

CHAPTER FIVE

STATIONS: FOOD AND LODGING ON THE TRAIL

S tage stops and stations were established at close intervals on the routes out west. They not only served as a place to rest and eat after or during a tiring journey but also as a point in which to change horses and drivers.

In Colorado, stations were located ten to twenty miles apart. The four main routes in Colorado were from Julesburg to Denver City, Denver City to Colorado City, Holly to Cañon City, and Denver City to Laramie, Wyoming. There were smaller routes located throughout the mountains to give access to the mining camps. The stations varied in terms of the services they provided and the condition of their buildings. Most of them had a couple of employees, but more important stations had up to six people working. Their primary duties included tending to the eighteen to twenty animals housed at the station, feeding the passengers, and changing teams when the stagecoach arrived.

There were generally two kinds of stations along the routes: the "swing" station and the "home" station. The swing station was usually a single building that housed the attendants. At this station, the passengers could stretch their legs for a few minutes while the teams were being changed. Swing stations on the plains were further apart than in the mountains — from twelve to twenty-five miles. A stage averaging six or seven miles an hour would make a stop every hour and a half or so.

The home stations were fifty to ninety miles apart on the plains and were usually the end of the route for the driver. The passengers had their

· AN EARLY STATION ON THE SOUTH PLATTE ·

A pen and ink drawing of an old stagecoach station on the South Platte.
Drawing by Steven M. Burke

meals at these stations, usually spending the night in local accommodations. When stagecoaching was in its infancy, stations were no more than tents, but, as time went on, more permanent structures were built. Most structures were built of log, adobe, or sod, depending on the materials available at the site. The size of the buildings varied also, the largest being comprised of three or four rooms, a kitchen/dining room, and two sleeping rooms. The smaller stations were usually square, incorporating large pieces of muslin as room dividers. To the traveler's dismay, there was very little privacy under such conditions.

The lives of station employees were dull but systematic. A stage departed about every ten hours, one from each end of the line. Because of all the potential problems, the managers didn't worry until a stage was over two hours late in arriving at any station along the route. When, from a distance, the station keepers could hear the approaching stage or see the dust on the horizon, they swung into action. The stock tenders harnessed the relief team and prepared for the coach's arrival.

The stations along the Platte River were aptly described in Frank A. Root's book, *An Overland Journey to California in 1879.*

> *There was a remarkable similarity in many of the stations along the Platte River on the Overland Stagelines for nearly 250 miles. Most of the buildings were built by the Stage Company, and*

usually were square, one-story hand hewn, cedar log structures of one to three rooms.

A log placed across from gable to gable supported the roof, by which poles were supported for rafters placed as close as they could be put together, side by side. On these were placed some willows, then a layer of hay was spread, and this was all covered with earth or sod; and lastly a sprinkling of course gravel or sand covered it all, to keep the earth from being blown off. The logs, which most stations were constructed of, were cut in the canyons south of the Platte, in the vicinity of Cottonwood Springs.

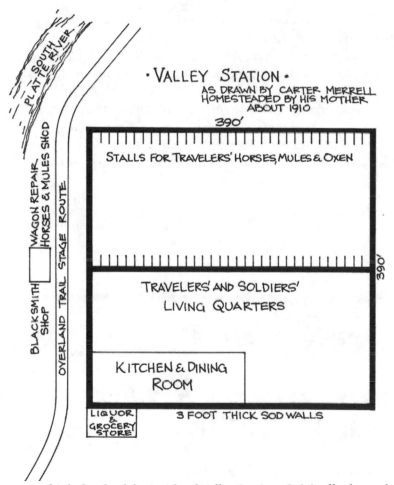

A pen and ink sketch of the inside of Valley Station. Originally drawn by Carter Merrell. Homesteaded by his mother about 1910.

Redrawn by Steven M. Burke

Nearly all of the swing stations along the entire line were similar in construction and looked much alike. A number of home stations, however, differed somewhat in several respects, being two to three times larger, and provided with sheds, outbuildings, and a number of other conveniences.

The station, stable and outbuildings at old Julesburg, for example, were built when that was the point where the through coaches forded the South Platte for Salt Lake City and California, going up the Rocky Ridge Road along Lodge Pole Creek. Besides being the point where the stages on the main line crossed the Platte, it also became an important junction for nearly four years.

Most of the stations east of Denver City for about a hundred miles were constructed of rough-cut lumber hauled from the mountains near the Platte Valley. The buildings were plain, the boards being of native Colorado Pine, nailed on the frame perpendicular.

There were about twenty-five regular eating stations on the line between Atchison and Denver City. Most of them were so well provided with conveniences that they could prepare a good meal on the shortest notice, better than might have been expected so far

Photo of a drawing of the Julesburg Number 2 stage stop in Julesburg, Colorado, in Sedgwick County. This may have been a depiction of Julesburg #2 shortly after the burning of Julesburg #1 by Indians, February 2, 1865.
Courtesy of Denver Public Library, Western History Collection 1867

out on the plains. The station keepers were more on giving passengers the necessities than the light and dainty delicacies. Being bounced from side to side on the coach while traveling over a rough road was sufficient reason to give almost any person an appetite for a solid, "square" meal.

Mark Twain described one station in his book, *Roughing It*, which was written in 1872.

> *You had to bend to get in the door. In place of a window there was a square hole just large enough for a man to crawl through but this did not have glass. There was no flooring, but the ground was hard packed. There were no shelves, no cupboards, and no closets. In a corner stood an open sack of flour, and nestling against its base were a couple of black tin coffeepots, a tin teapot, a little bag of salt and a side of bacon. The furniture was sparse. The rocking chairs and sofas were not present, and never had been, but two three-legged stools, a pine board bench four feet long, and two empty candleholders represented them. The table was a greasy board on stilts, and the tablecloth and napkins had not arrived and they were not looking for them either.*

Latham was a prominent eating stage station associated with the Overland Trail. The station was near the mouth of the Cache le Poudre River — about thirty-five miles from the eastern edge of the mountains — on the old Cherokee Trail, which entered the mountains at Laporte. The station was sixty miles northeast of Denver City.

The station was the only house in sight, and there wasn't another one for three-quarters of a mile in any direction. In a radius of ten miles from Latham, there were no more than ten houses, and ranchers occupied all of these. It was very desolate.

Mr. W.S. McIlwain, a genial, warm-hearted man, was the stage company agent at Latham, and he also maintained the eating station. With the help of his wife and Miss Lizzie Trout, whose services as cook were hired out at ten dollars a week, he gained a reputation for providing one of the best eating houses on the entire line.

Prominent as Latham was in 1864, it was virtually unknown by 1879. Most people living in Weld County have never heard of the station, which was closed five years before Weld County was created. But in its day, there were frequently as many as three stages (coming from Atchison, California, and Denver City) standing in front of Latham Station.

This stagecoach inn was located near the top of Mosquito Pass on the stage road between Fairplay and Leadville. This inn was operated from 1879 until 1890. It was moved to South Park City without losing any of the original chinking between the logs.

Courtesy of South Park City

In the 1860s, the warmest buildings along the Platte in the winter and the coolest in the summer were constructed of either sod or adobe, usually called "doby." During the Indian troubles on the plains in 1864 and 1865, these buildings were relatively safe against Indian attacks. Most had strong, massive walls two or three feet wide. Although the walls were constructed to be fireproof, they also served exceptionally well at deflecting bullets. Likewise, it is said that all such buildings were capable of withstanding even the strongest windstorms that swept across the plains. Those who had spent most of their lives on the frontier believed them to be cyclone-proof, declaring that nothing short of an earthquake could knock them down.

Another prominent stage station in 1862 was Virginia Dale. Jack and Virginia Slade, along with many other stageline employees, called it their home. This station was busy at all times, with coaches arriving and departing during all hours of the day and night. Employees were kept busy preparing meals for the travelers, making ready for possible Indian attacks, and dealing with extreme weather events, such as blinding snowstorms, torrential rains, and piercing windstorms.

CHAPTER 5: STATIONS

Virginia Dale had an active social life, as did many of the larger stations. Settlers and ranchers from miles around gathered frequently for dances and social interaction. Some of the station's employees played the fiddle or guitar, and dances often lasted all night long. Virginia Dale did not have a piano, because it would have to have been hauled hundreds of miles by a freight company, although many other stations did not spare even this expense. The quadrille and the Virginia reel were the favorite dances of the time.

Hay and grain were harvested from nearby lush meadows to help supply the warehouses at Virginia Dale. They were usually well-prepared for hungry passengers, too — stocking canned and dried fruits and smoked meats before winter set in. With hundreds of animals and passengers coming and going, large amounts of supplies had to be stored. Supply wagons arrived regularly to deliver goods to Virginia Dale and other stations on the route.

The Virginia Dale Stage Station was built in 1862 and is a remarkable example of a hand-hewn log building. In 1985, the stage station was designated on the *National Register of Historic Properties*. In early 1996, funding was granted from the Colorado Historical Society to stabilize and preserve the building. It is the only surviving stage station on the Overland Trail and remains an irreplaceable link to our western heritage.

Waneka Station, built by Adolph Waneka in the early 1860s, was a two-story stone structure that served as both a ranch house and stage stop. Passengers traveling from Denver City to Cheyenne and from Fort Collins to Denver City stopped at Waneka Station for food and lodging.

On the Denver City to Cheyenne route, another station, built in 1863 by Mary and Lafayette Miller, was called the Rock Creek Stage Station. Mrs. Miller, known for her inviting meals, was asked in the summer of 1867 if she could feed a circus troupe that would arrive soon. It was said that she set to work cooking, eventually serving hot, tasty meals to 100 performers from the John Robinson Circus (the first circus to perform in Colorado).

On a hillside near Lamar and Springfield is a unique, plain, sandstone ranch house known historically as the Petticrew Ranch. Surrounded by sandstone outcroppings, native prairie grass, and yucca, the ranch served as the Petticrew Stage Station. The ranch building still appears much like it did in the 1890s, with dry-stacked stonewalls and a sod-covered roof. The unique barn is an example of the stone bank design and was used for freight wagons and stagecoach horses.

There were many other stations along the route between Denver City and Latham — Big Bend, Fort Lupton, Pierson's, Church's, Boone's, St. Vrain, Little Thompson, Namaqua, Spring Creek, Sherwood, and Laporte.

A BUMPY RIDE

Denver's Four-Mile House filled an important need as a wayside inn, tavern, and stage stop in the 1860s. The house was built along the old Cherokee Trail in 1859. The trail, once used by woodland Indians, traders, and trappers, linked the trading posts on the South Platte River with the Santa Fe Trail and Bent's Fort. Travelers found Four-Mile House to be a pleasant diversion from uncomfortable and monotonous stage travel. Here, tired teams were exchanged for fresh ones before traversing the last few miles into Denver City.

Four-Mile House continued to be the stop for Denver City and Santa Fe coaches until about 1870, when the railroad was built into Denver. The old road no longer exists, having been plowed under, planted over, and washed away by the raging floods that have always plagued Cherry Creek.

Unknown to many Coloradoans is the Four-Mile Historic Park. On December 20, 1968, Four-Mile House was designated a Denver Landmark, and, on December 2, 1969, it was listed on the National Register of Historic Places. It is open to the public.

About ten miles from Golden was a station called the Guy House. John C. Guy from Boston built this stage station in the summer of 1859. The station was especially noteworthy because it sat on the west side of Guy

View of a stagecoach at a frame hotel in Blackhawk, Gilpin County, Colorado; also shows people and buggies circa 1862.
Courtesy of Denver Public Library, Western History Collection

View from hill down into Guy Gulch, a stage stop in Jefferson County, Colorado, shows a few horse-drawn stagecoaches and wagons in front of a large wood frame residence with picket fence, outhouse, and several outbuildings nestled in a narrow gulch. (Between 1870 and 1900)
Courtesy of Denver Public Library, Western History Collection

Hill and was reached by a very steep, winding road. Guy House station is reported to have provided the best accommodations available in the territory and was a welcome sight to weary travelers.

Guy House became a valuable piece of property and was sold nearly every year to a new owner. The station property included a fine hotel with excellent food and lodging, corrals, barns, and a blacksmith shop. Sturdy animals were kept there for pulling heavy loads up the west side of Guy Hill. Guy House was frequently advertised in the *Rocky Mountain News* and in local mining camp newspapers, but no record has ever been found as to what eventually happened to it.

Eight-Mile House was located eight miles from Golden. In 1899, Henry and Matilda Ramstetter moved to the stage stop on the Golden Gate

Canyon Road. As the main route between Central City and Blackhawk, the house served as an important stage stop in the region.

Eight Mile stage stop had two stories and featured a huge kitchen, dining room, parlor, and three bedrooms. As was quite common in those days, there was a cellar dug into the hillside adjoining the kitchen. The cellar housed canned and dried vegetables and meats, like a family's own private grocery store. On the top floor, there was a large hall with six windows on the west side and two windows on the south. The property also had many outbuildings, such as barns, granaries, pigpens, and corrals. A smokehouse and slaughtering shed completed the ranch. Jefferson County records show that, in 1860, Thomas M. Robinson built the house, and it was soon deeded over to Robinson-Baker Co.

Daniel Booten built Centennial House, located twelve miles from Golden on the Golden Gate Canyon Road, in 1876 (there was reportedly a stone over the front door with the date of 1876 inscribed on it). It was located two miles north of the Guy House and was used as a stage stop for many years.

The Pullman House stood for one hundred and six years and in 1965 was one of the oldest remaining buildings still standing in Colorado. It was built near Golden in the fall of 1859. Pullman and Associates bought the house in 1860 and combined it with other properties to form the Cold Springs Ranch. It became one of the more famous stage stations in Colorado Territory. The house was enlarged many times and was used for different purposes over the years. It began as a station for stage-coaches, wagons, trains, and finally was used by persons traveling in automobiles.

In 1965, the *Rocky Mountain News* and *The Denver Post* reported that the historical old building was to be destroyed. A sad time, to be sure, for Pullman House. Later, it was reported that the new owner dismantled and numbered each log as it was being torn down and moved it to Central City. No one seems to know if it was ever rebuilt.

In 1870, Samuel Houghland built an adobe and log structure that became an important stage stop and was used to service stagecoaches and freight wagons as they traveled west from Saguache over Old Cochetopa Pass to and from the Los Pinos Indian Agency, Lake City, and Gunnison. In 1889, Sam received help from the family of Pete Phillips in the operation of his business. Dances were frequently held in the old building, which also was used as a boarding house until 1917. When Highway 114 over North Pass was paved, it was reported that the road crew stayed in the old stage stop, but by the time the automobiles arrived on the scene, the stage stop had ceased to operate.

CHAPTER 5: STATIONS

In 1981, John Cumby, a summer resident of Gunnison, purchased the old building from the Saguache Flickinger family. The building was dismantled and rebuilt just eighteen miles north of Gunnison and was finally recognized as a Colorado Historical Site in March of 1983.

Near Steamboat Springs, there was another "Rock Creek Stage Stop." The stop was a unique two-story structure that may have been built in stages, as the first floor and second floor were constructed in a manner noticeably different from each other. After crossing Gore Pass, passengers and horses rested at the Rock Creek Stage Stop. In the 1870s, Wells Fargo and Co. carried mail destined for the Yampa Valley. Rock Creek Stage Stop was a one-day trip from Steamboat Springs through Toponas and Oak Creek. From that point, the trail divided and ventured south to State Bridge. In the high mountain meadows along the route, the stage company kept corrals where tired horses could spend a few days eating mountain hay and native meadow grass.

After the stagecoaching era, the Rock Creek Stage Station operated as both a service center for settlers and a shelter for travelers in the 1930s. In 2000, the station had become so run down that the Colorado Preservation, Inc., named it one of Colorado's most endangered places.

Margaret Long, M.D., wrote a unique historical book entitled *Automobile Logs of the Smoky Hill Trail in 1943*. It details the route of the Smoky Hill Trail in mileage increments, and Dr. Long describes in great detail how to follow the trail. She begins one log in Cheyenne Wells at 0.0 miles:

> At 7.5 miles, you will cross the Smoky Hill Trail. An arrow on the south side of the highway points southward along the line of the Smoky Hill Trail, which can be seen going toward Eureka Station. This station is one and a half miles from this reading. At 10.9 miles on the odometer you will reach Eureka Stage Station site at the trail crossing the gulch.
>
> From Wild Horse to Hugo on U. S. Highway 40, you begin at Wild Horse at 0.0 miles and travel west on Highway 40. At 17.3 miles there are some sheds southwest of this corner. Connell Creek Station site is southeast of the section corner. The tracks of the Smoky Hill Trail can be seen on this hillside on both sides of the creek.
>
> The Smoky Hill north runs through unsettled country and is preserved practically all the way from Cheyenne Wells to Hugo. From Deering's Well, you drive 9.2 miles taking down and replacing barbed wire fences as you go. As near as can be determined this is a stage station site. The only trace of it is a small bare spot,

*surrounded by a low embankment covered with Buffalo grass. The
site is on the slope above the west bank of the creek.*

This is a fascinating and unusual book, listing old stage stations like
old Julesburg, Gittrell's Ranch, Antelope Station, Buffalo Springs Ranch,
Spring Hill Station, Lillian Spring, Dennison's Ranch, and Valley Station
in Sterling.

Along the stagecoach routes, home stations were where passengers slept
and took their meals. There were many negative reports of meals served
and services performed along the trail. One traveler complained, "The uni-
formity of the food, fried bacon and hot biscuits, the latter yellow with
soda, gave no indication as to whether we were eating breakfast, lunch or
supper."

Various locations did, however, serve different kinds of foods. The
menus and the quality and quantity of food quite often depended on the
cook's tastes and abilities. Meals between Julesburg and Denver City often
featured ham, dried pork, and canned fruit. At Boone's Station, travelers
were often served venison or beef, fresh fruit, vegetables, and milk or coffee; however, after a fresh kill of wild game, stations often served venison
and bear meat three times a day.

*This stagecoach Inn was originally near the top of Mosquito Pass. South Park
City, Colorado, did an authentic restoration of an early mining town. 1860*
Courtesy of South Park Historical Foundation

CHAPTER 5: STATIONS

William W. Taylor managed Laporte Station, located six miles north of Fort Collins. The cook was Taylor's wife, and she became famous on the stagelines in Colorado. She was an expert at preparing an excellent table, featuring such delicacies as dried apples and beans.

In Mark Twain's book, *Roughing It,* he describes the food and beverages he encountered at stages stations along the route.

> *The station cook sliced off a piece of bacon for each man, but only experienced old timers made out to eat it, as it was condemned army bacon which the United States would not feed its soldiers at the forts and the stage company had bought it cheap for the sustenance of their passengers and employees. We may have found this condemned army bacon further out on the plains than the section I am in, but we found it, nonetheless.*
>
> *Then he poured a beverage called "Slumgullion," and it is hard to think he was not inspired when he named it. It pretty much tasted like tea, but there was too much dishrag, sand, and old bacon rind in it to deceive the intelligent traveler. We had no sugar and no milk, not even a spoon to stir the ingredients with.*
>
> *We could not eat the bread or meat, nor drink the slumgullion. And when I looked at that melancholy vinegar cruet, I thought of the old anecdote (a very, very old one, even at this day), of the traveler who sat down to the table which had nothing on it but mackerel and a pot of mustard. The landlord was asked if that was all there was, and the landlord replied, "All! Why thunder and lightening, I should think there was enough mackerel there for six." "But I don't like mackerel," said the traveler, "Oh, then help yourself to the mustard."*
>
> *Our breakfast was before us, but our teeth were idle. I tasted and smelt, and I said I would take coffee, I believed. The station boss stopped dead still, and glared at me speechless.*
>
> *We could not eat, and there was no conversation among the hostlers and herdsmen, though we all sat at the same table. At least there was no conversation further than a single harried request, now and then, from one employee to another. It was always the same form, and always gruffly friendly. Its western freshness and novelty startled me, at first, and interested me, but it presently grew monotonous, and lost its charm.*

On the stage, travelers often carried with them the most offensive foods. Sardines, strong cheese, herring, and bologna were not uncommon.

Crull/Hammond Cabin Project. In 2002, Wallace E. Carroll, Jr., donated this historic cabin and surrounding land to Douglas County with hopes that a restoration could be undertaken. A partnership with the Larkspur Historical Society, Douglas County Historic Preservation Board, and Douglas County enabled the project to begin in 2004. This site was homesteaded by William Crull, the first postmaster of Huntsville, on November 12, 1870, and is significant in Douglas County History. Huntsville was Douglas County's first territorial post office and stage stop for early travelers and freighters along Plum Creek.

Photo by Author

Stations farthest from the division centers seldom served fresh vegetables, fruits, or milk, usually providing only thin coffee, fried salt pork, or hard biscuits. Prices of meals on the main stageline varied from fifty cents to over two dollars. The farther west a person went, the more expensive the prices became. In 1863, a dozen eggs at Latham was $1.25, while coffee and butter was $1.00 a pound.

There were a few stations that sunk to an even lower level of service, and they were more than even a driver who had spent the greater part of his life on the box could stand. Some of them were indescribably filthy, even by the standards of an overland station far out on the frontier — for no one ever expected that all the necessities and comforts of life could be obtained at an overland eating establishment. At one station in particular, it was observed that one of the drivers frequently played sick; he couldn't eat, he said, because of a weak stomach. He had for some time been hanging around the house and noticed the cook fondling the dogs and cats and then, without washing her hands, thrust them into a sack of flour to mix up a pan of biscuits. The driver would rather go hungry and wait until he reached the next station, than attempt to eat after watching the process of how the food was prepared.

According to Frank A. Root's book *The Overland Stage to California*, food and lodging often weren't up to decent standards.

> *Along the South Platte west of Fort Kearney, for a considerable distance, we for weeks had nothing in the pastry line except dried apple pie. This article of diet for dessert became so plentiful that the drivers and stock tenders rebelled, but the passengers also joined in, some of them "kicking" like government mules. As a few of the drivers expressed it, it was "dried apple pie from Genesis to Revelations." Finally this flowing poem, author unknown, which very soon had the desired effect, was copied and sent on it way east and west up and down the Platte.*

> *Dried Apple Pie*
> *I Loathe! Abhor! Distaste! Despise!*
> *Abominate dried apple pies;*
> *I like good bread; I like good meat,*
> *Or anything that's good to eat;*

> *But of all poor grub beneath the skies*
> *The poorest is dried apple pies.*
> *Give me a toothache or sore eyes,*
> *In preference to such kind of pies.*

> *The farmer takes his gangliest fruit*
> *'Tis wormy, bitter, and hard, to boot,*
> *They leave the hulls to make us cough*
> *And don't take half the peelings off.*

> *Then on a dirty cord they're strung,*
> *And there they serve a roost for flies,*
> *Until they're ready to make pies.*

> *Tread on my corns, or tell me lies,*
> *But don't pass me dried-apple pies.*

In the spring of 1874, being hungry for fresh fruit, and noticing some apples at one of the stores in Denver City that looked tempting, I bought a couple for which I paid twenty-five cents each. They were Missouri Pippins, a wagonload of them having been hauled by a farmer from Buchanan County, Missouri, about 700 miles across the plains, to the metropolis of the new gold region. The apples quickly found a market, and they netted the freighter a very handsome profit.

At Latham Station, sixty miles below Denver City, on the South Platte, I bought, a few months later, one dozen extra-choice apricots, that were brought from Salt Lake City, 600 miles across the Rockies by overland stage express, for which I paid three dollars in greenbacks, and thought at the time that I was getting a bargain.

The canned fruits now so common all over the country were almost unknown on the plains in the early 1860s. The finest dried fruits we had at Latham station, the latter part of 1863, and for over nine months in 1864 were peaches, grown, dried and brought from Salt Lake City. While they cost fully twice as much as the kind that came from the east, they were well worth it, for they were as much superior in flavor to the eastern dried peach as the latter in every way except the gnarliest dried apple.

The finest meal I ate in Denver City, a Sunday dinner at the Planter's Hotel (The Overland Stageline headquarters), was between three and four hours after my arrival in the city on January 29, 1863. I have thought, and think to this day, that it was one of the finest meals I ever sat down to in Colorado. The genial Col. James McNassar, a prince among landlords, kept the house at the time. An elaborate bill of fare had been prepared, to which ample justice was done by the very large number of guests. Among the articles of food were mountain trout, buffalo, roast wild turkey, chicken, duck and grouse.

The Planter's Hotel was a two-story frame structure, but it was then considered the only first-class hotel in the city of Denver, taking in guests a full three-fourths of the traveling public. McNassar was one of the most hospitable landlords in the Rocky Mountain region, and he was highly esteemed as a citizen of Denver City. When he retired from the Planter's, John Hughes, a prominent citizen and popular hotelkeeper, succeeded him. The historic Planter's Hotel, which stood for about a quarter of a century as one of the early landmarks of the Rocky Mountain metropolis, was torn down to make room for a more imposing and substantial building.

CHAPTER 5: STATIONS

View of people, horses and covered wagons on a dirt street in Denver, Colorado. Shows men, carriages, and wagons in front of the Planter's House Building, a two-story, frame hotel and stage stop at the corner of 16th street and Blake in downtown Denver. Women hold parasols and stand on a balcony below a sign that reads: "Overland Stage Line."
1864 Image, Courtesy of Colorado Historical Society CHS-X4774

In 1876, Ouray was in dire need of a substantial hotel and stage stop. That spring, James and Mary Dixon arrived in Ouray with that very thought in mind. They would build one on the northwest corner of Fourth Street and Sixth Avenue, where the community center is today. In only two short years after the hotel opened, James Dixon, age forty-four, passed away, leaving his widow alone in the little frontier town of Ouray. However, only a few months passed before Mary began planning for expansion. First, she added dormer windows on the second floor, which was pretty common in hotels of that era. She also added fourteen large, well-ventilated sleeping rooms for the employees above the dining room.

Mary Dixon borrowed money on August 14, 1881, to help pay for this renovation; but, lo and behold, she could not repay the loan, and so the hotel was sold to the highest bidder, Louis King, for $5,684.00.

On June 4, 1892, fifteen years after it was built, a dreaded thing happened. A kitchen fire started about four o'clock in the afternoon and

Hotel Dixon in Ouray, Colorado. Notice the three stagecoaches waiting for their passengers in front of the hotel. This hotel burned down in 1892.
Courtesy of Charlie Hosner Collection, Montrose, Colorado

rapidly spread to the sleeping apartments above. Due to the quick action of the fire department, some of the hotel was saved. But, two months later, another fire totally burned the Dixon Hotel to the ground. The local newspapers headlines reported, "Old Landmark Gone."

The Western Mountaineer, *December 6, 1860*

Current Prices
Collected weekly for the Mountaineer
By W. A. H. Loveland and Co.
Washington Avenue, Golden City

Groceries and Provisions

Bacon	*35 cents per pound*
Beans	*10 cents per pound*
Butter	*60 cents per pound*
Lard	*30 cents per pound*
Sugar	*25 cents per pound*
Eggs	*50 cents per dozen*

CHAPTER 5: STATIONS

Western Mountaineer, *December 6, 1860*

Jefferson House
Washington Ave., Golden City
O. B. Harvey, Proprietor

The proprietor respectfully informs his friends and the public generally, that he is still to be found at his old stand, ready to cater for their welfare and hopes to receive a share of public patronage. He flatters himself that those sojourning with him, will find his house a pleasant and comfortable retreat, and thinks that he can and will endeavor to please, so as to render entire satisfaction. Also, in connection with the house, a large and commodious stable is available.

There is a daily line of stagecoaches running to and from the house, to all parts of the country.

Kenosha House was a stage station at the west side of Kenosha Hill. It was built in the early 1860s and was still operating in the late 1890s. This picture was taken in 1870.

Courtesy of The South Park Historical Foundation

CHAPTER SIX

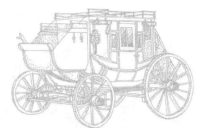

ROBBERS, THIEVES, AND OUTLAWS

Acry of "Halt! Throw down your guns!" or "Hold up your hands and don't move!" meant only one thing in the frontier west of the 1880s. When the Indian uprisings gradually began to end, the stageline employees confronted a new adversary. With a gun pointing at the back of their head, few passengers and drivers ever argued with the bands of dangerous thieves they sometimes encountered. Travelers in those days knew many dangers were possible as they rode across the mountains and plains, but none as terrifying as being at the mercy of a gang of desperadoes.

As Frank A. Root described in his book *An Overland Journey to California*, there were many interesting episodes and hair's breadth escapes. Even Ben Holladay, the proprietor of the great Overland Stageline, was caught unaware when the coach he was riding in was held up at gunpoint.

> One night I was bouncing over the plains in one of my overland coaches. Mrs. Holladay and myself were the only passengers. Several stages had been robbed within two months, and the driver was ripping along as though a gang of prairie wolves were after him. Suddenly, the horses were thrown on their haunches and the stage stopped. I was heaved forward, but quickly recovered, and found myself gazing into the muzzle of a double-barreled shotgun.
>
> "Throw up your hands and don't stir!" shouted the owner, in a gruff voice. Up went my hands and I began to commune with

myself. The fellow then coolly asked for my money. I saw that he did not know who I was, and I was afraid that my sick wife might awaken and call my name. My coat was buttoned over my bosom, but scarcely high enough to hide a magnificent emerald that cost me over $8000.00 a few weeks ago in San Francisco. I scarcely breathed through fear that light might strike the stone, and its sparkling brilliancy might attract the attention of the robber. I had about $40,000.00 in a money belt and several hundred dollars in my pockets.

Suddenly the robber shouted, "Come on, shell out quick, or I'll send the old 'un a free lunch." I passed out the few hundreds loose in my pocket and handed him my gold watch and chain. They were heavy, I think the chain alone would weigh five pounds.

I said, "There's every cent I've got! Take it and let me go. My wife is very ill, and I don't know what would happen to her if she knew what was going on."

"Keep your hands up!" was the reply, while a second robber took my watch and money. Then a search was made for the express company's box, but the double-barreled shotgun did not move. Its muzzles were within a foot of my nose. For my life, I did not dare to stir. My nose began to itch. The stiff hairs of my mustache got up and one after the other tickled it, until the sensation was intolerable. I could stand it no longer.

"Stranger," I said, "I must scratch my nose! It itches so bad that I'm almost crazy." "Move your hands" he shouted, "and I'll blow a hole through your head big enough for a jack rabbit to jump through!"

I appealed to him once more. "Well," he answered, "Keep your hands still and I'll scratch it for you." "Did he scratch it?" asked one of Ben's interested listeners. "Sure," said Mr. Holladay. "How?" asked the breathless listener. "With the muzzle of the loaded gun," said the great overlander. "He rubbed the muzzle around my mustache and raked it over the end of my nose, until I thanked him and said that it itched no longer."

The robbers soon afterwards took their leave, with many apologies, and I continued my journey to the Missouri River, along with the big emerald and my $40,000.00.

Uncle Dick Wooten, a bearded old mountain man who owned a road-house and stage stop on Raton Pass, had let the fire die out, believing that the stagecoach with all of its passengers would not be stopping in at such

*With the stagecoach came the stagecoach robbery. Here, an Eastern dandy is being stripped of his valuables by some rough-looking customers near Leadville, Colorado, in the early 1880s. (*Frank Leslie's Illustrated Newspaper, *November 11, 1882)*

Courtesy of P. David Smith

a late hour. He lay in the darkness and thought about how successful his toll road and stage stop had become. It was quite an undertaking to blast out the rocks and build the log bridges needed to complete his toll road. He had had to acquire permission from two territories, New Mexico and Colorado, just to be able to begin its construction.

He built the road so that it followed an old Indian trail over Raton Pass. In 1858, he drove a whole wagonload of supplies over the trail, where before the only possible way to travel was by horseback. It took him over a month to travel fifty miles because he had to literally chop his way through the trees.

In 1865, his dirt road was finally completed, and it became a very busy thoroughfare. Stagecoaches carrying passengers, mail, and army troops; freighters with wagonloads of goods bound for New Mexico; Mexicans; and Indians all traversed the toll road.

Because of the great cost involved in building the road, he made it a toll road, whereby he would be able to collect money to help pay for his expenses. Most of the travelers paid willingly and went on their way; however, every now and then, a troublemaker would argue that he shouldn't have to pay. When someone pointed a gun at them, they usually changed their minds. When officers of the law were on the trail of cattle or horse thieves, they were not expected to pay — nor were Indians traveling from one of their camps to another.

Just as Uncle Dick was falling asleep, he heard a loud scuffling noise and the tinkle of broken glass. He ran to the window and saw some men sneaking out of the bar next door. The Ross Gang! They were headed straight toward him, so Uncle Dick grabbed his rifle, thrust it through a broken windowpane, and shouted; "Halt, or I'll shoot!"

The robbers, surprised by this action, stopped short. Jack Ross, the gang leader, said, "Sorry to disturb your sleep, partner, but it does get mighty cold and lonesome around these parts at night. My friends and I have a long and chilly ride ahead of us. How about letting us in, so we can bed down for the night?"

"Sorry, boys, but you're out of luck," shouted Uncle Dick. "I know who you are and what you're up to, and I have no intention of opening up to a gang of no-goods at this hour of the night. I'm gonna give you thirty seconds to return that liquor and clear out of here, or I'll blow your brains out! Now, how's that for western hospitality?"

The Ross Gang grabbed their horses and fled. About then, Uncle Dick heard the midnight stage rumbling down the mountain. The Ross Gang was going to hold up Uncle Dick and then the stagecoach full of passengers. When the stage pulled up to Uncle Dick's station, he warned them about the Ross Gang and loaned a few extra firearms to the passengers, who never did meet up with the robbers, as they hurried on toward Trinidad.

Jim Reynolds was a miner in California Gulch, later known as Leadville. He got approval from the Colorado Governor to travel to Texas, his home state, to get a regiment together for the Union Army. Many people thought he was good-hearted and honest to attempt such an endeavor. Soon enough, though, they learned that the "regiment" was up to no good and, instead of helping the government, were working only to benefit themselves.

When he arrived on the Platte River, Reynolds had eight men and nine excellent horses. Reynolds and his gang held up the stagecoach owned by Billy Berry, Ad Williamson, and Bob Spottswood. A young girl who had saved $400 by working at the Fairplay Hotel was one of the passengers. Showing a nasty and merciless attitude, they took all of her money. Another passenger, Mr. Dunbar, thinking that he could outsmart the bandits, grabbed a whiskey bottle and pretended to be drunk. The bandits, thinking that he was just a hopeless drunk, left him alone. Unbeknownst to them, he was the wealthiest of all the passengers.

CHAPTER 6: ROBBERS, THIEVES AND OUTLAWS

The Denver City citizens formed a posse, and those who were chosen proceeded in hot pursuit of the gang. The outlaws were camped on the South Platte River below South Park. They were well hidden in the timber, and, knowing that they would be followed, they hid the loot in a well-chosen spot along the road. Some say the buried treasure was found shortly after Jim Reynolds execution, while others are still searching for it today.

In September of 1880, two masked men robbed the stage just west of Ohio City, taking only the mailbags. There was an ill passenger aboard at the time, but the road agents did not rob him. However, the driver, Jack Hansborough, was getting tired of this routine, as he had already been robbed six times.

Sometimes, on a slow news day, the newspapers tended to stretch the truth somewhat. This story appeared in the *White Pine Cone*, on February 15, 1889.

Last Monday was favorable for a tragedy. For some time dark clouds hid the sun, and a snowfall darkened the heavens. The atmosphere was gruesome and uncanny. A feeling of depression came over the passengers, a silent premonition of approaching danger.

Sitting beside and near the driver, Ingold Peterson, were Joe Domandel, Miss Lily Dinkins and an alleged drummer. Let us say right here that the drummer was suspicious. It is even charged directly that he was an accomplice of the hold-up and an accessory before the fact.

When the stage stopped in Cosden, he was seen going into Pat's place and emerged a few minutes later with a strong aroma on his breath. Was this a signal to his pal, watching from the trees?

He frequently glanced at the mailbags and nervously watched on either side of the road when the canyon was approached. It was particularly noticed that just before the stage was attacked, the drummer placed his thumb and forefinger to his nose almost as a signal.

Evidently the drummer should have been apprehended. Witnesses can be produced who will swear they saw the road agent throw something, which the drummer caught with a dexterity that comes with long practice. About midway between Cosden and White Pine, as the driver hurried the team around the curve in the road, there suddenly came into view a dark, grim sentinel, who stood silently by the side of the road. He did not speak, but his actions were ominous and the passengers shuddered as the stage drew near.

Joe Domandel, having the safety of a lady at heart, begged the driver to stop, but the blood of the Northman was aroused and like warrior chieftains of his ancestry, he resolved to do or die.

A few sharp screams, mutters and stifling gasps and the danger was past, but the robber had done his work. The driver and a passenger had been badly injured as the faithful horses brought the stage into White Pine. It was known here the moment the stage came into sight that an accident had occurred. There was something in the air that spoke of catastrophe. A nervous crowd gathered as the stage approached.

The robber escaped and the drummer disappeared. The driver and passenger recovered but vowed to yell at the first sight of such a mean, low-down loaded skunk.

There was a young Swedish girl named Huldah, who boarded the stage at Lake City to make the journey to Denver City. It was there she was to meet her "sweetheart" as soon as he arrived from the "old country." She had endured the backbreaking chore of doing laundry for the miners for enough months to save up the money for her wedding dress. On this fateful day, her costume included a broad brim straw hat. At the bottom of a very steep hill, the passengers were asked to get out and walk up the hill to spare the horses.

Huldah and the male passengers on the coach complied with the request. Just as they began their long trek up the hill, a gust of wind took off her straw hat and deposited it at the top of an old, dead tree. Huldah was hysterical and pleaded with the men to get it back for her. They assured her that they would buy her a new one when they reached Denver City. Huldah burst into tears and confessed to the men that her life savings of $1,000 was sewn into the lining of the hat. Feeling sorry for Huldah, one of the passengers got the hat down off the dead tree by using the stage driver's whip, much to her delight.

Everything seemed to be going along fine until just before dark, when three masked men held up the stage. There wasn't as much loot as they had expected, so the robbers, arguing among themselves, considered taking the government strongbox. This was not simply fun to them anymore, however, because they could then be prosecuted for tampering with the United States mail.

Just then, a passenger named Bennett pointed to the young girl and exclaimed, "that girl has $1,000 sewn into her hat." They were pleased to get the $1,000 and rode off into the night. The government strongbox was safe, but Bennett was in a world of trouble. The other men were angry with Bennett for betraying the girl and threatened to hang him on the spot. He had to do a lot of fast-talking to get out of this mess. He promised that when they reached Denver City, he would give Huldah the money that was stolen from her.

When they reached Denver City, Bennett, accompanied by the determined passengers, opened the strongbox and retrieved the money he had deposited in it at the beginning of the journey: $40,000! He not only repaid Huldah the money that was stolen from her hat, but also bought her a beautiful trousseau. When Huldah's sweetheart arrived to claim his happy bride, she greeted him in the most beautiful dress money could buy.

Any society has to cope with the subject of crime. Many crimes in the frontier West went unpunished because of a lack of law enforcement of any kind. There were many real hazards of traveling by stagecoach in the West. In 1879, Slumgullion Pass, no more than a very rough wagon road, was the main route from Lake City to Del Norte (when the railroad reached Gunnison, it caused a shift in the routes of stagecoaches, freight, and mail to that town).

An escaped convict from a Detroit prison, Billy Le Roy, was about as dangerous an outlaw as the West had ever seen. Billy Le Roy, in order to avoid arrest, headed for the western frontier. His brother, Frank Clark, was waiting for him in Del Norte, Colorado.

In May of 1881, Le Roy, Clark, and another outlaw held up the Slumgullion stage just out of Del Norte. They robbed the passengers of most of their worldly goods, especially money and jewelry. The Barlow & Sanderson coach had a high-strung lead horse. When the outlaws shouted and waved their pistols in the air, it frightened the lead horse, and a runaway stagecoach was the result.

Sheriff L.M. Armstrong, along with James P. Galloway, formed a posse to apprehend the gang in the mountains. A reward of $1400 had been offered for the arrest of the Le Roy gang. The posse finally caught up with them and immediately took them to jail in Del Norte. Billy Le Roy was shot in the leg during the course of his arrest. Thinking that all was right with the world, Sheriff Armstrong headed toward home to get some well-deserved rest.

Local citizens had other ideas, however. During the middle of the night, the members of the Le Roy gang were taken from their cells to a clump of cottonwood trees near the jail, where they were then hanged. Robberies drastically declined along the Lake Fork and Slumgullion route for several months thereafter.

A rather unusual robbery occurred on June 2, 1881, when the westbound stage was held up three miles out of Pagosa Springs. The outlaws took $350 from one passenger and seventeen dollars from a young man. After talking it over, they returned two dollars to the young man because they thought he might have greater need of it than the wealthier gentleman. The only other passenger was a lady. She was not robbed, but they opened her trunk and removed some ladies' stockings. One of the outlaws thought that the stockings would be good for his sore leg because they were large and warm.

"Doc" Cyrus Wells Shores, who was a well-known sheriff of Gunnison County between 1884 and 1892, told the story of an unusual stage robber. When he wrote his memoirs, he included a tale about a man he called a "friend."

> Jim Clark came to Telluride in 1887. He got a job helping to dig a pipeline into town. This was a difficult job because the only way in those days was with a pick and shovel.
>
> Telluride was wide open and full of bad men who had the authorities buffaloed. They would often get drunk and shoot up the town, but the city Marshal, who was afraid of them, did not interfere.
>
> Clark soon sized up the situation and one day when a bunch of gunmen were terrorizing the town, he walked into the mayor's office and said, "If you give me a special appointment as deputy city marshall, I'll go out and arrest them fellers for you. It's about time that we had a little peace and quiet in this man's town." "They're pretty mean," the mayor answered, "but you look big enough to give them a run for their money. Go ahead and see what you can do. I'll stand behind you."
>
> By evening the jail was full of bewildered prisoners, and for the first time in its comparatively short history, the town was strangely quiet. Telluride had taken on the aspects of a peaceful, law-abiding community.
>
> Although quick as lightening on the draw and probably the best shot in Colorado, Clark did not find it necessary to use his guns that day. When any boisterous gunman started to draw on Clark, he knocked them down with his fists and took the gun away from him.
>
> The mayor and the city council were so impressed by Clark's efficient work that they immediately made him City Marshall, which job he still had when I first met him.
>
> I had been told that while Clark rigorously kept the peace in Telluride and wouldn't stand for any disorderliness whatsoever, he continued his own life of lawlessness outside of the city limits by disguising himself and participating in stagecoach holdups. It was rumored that he often tipped off his outlaw partners when a big gold or silver shipment was going out on the stagecoach from Telluride to the nearest rail head at Dallas, three miles below the present day Ridgway, and Clark would receive his cut from the holdups.

After hearing so much about this legendary Telluride marshal, I had wanted to meet him for a long time and find out what the real Jim Clark was like. This was my opportunity.

Jim Clark and I spent a good deal of time tracking down the Grand Junction train robbers (where they became acquainted). When Clark was about to leave Gunnison I said, "Why don't you leave your man here for a couple of days and go down with me to Cimarron to check on some cattle rustling?" "Why, I'd be glad to, Doc," he said, "You helped me out, (by assisting him in catching a horse thief) and maybe now I can return the favor. By the way, I want to show you something." He unbuttoned his shirt and pulled a roll of bills from a secret pocket sewn into the waist of his underwear.

"This was my cut out of the Telluride Bank Robbery," he said confidentially, removing a hundred-dollar bill and replacing the roll. Let's get this bill changed and I'll buy you a box of cigars."

"Well, Jim," I said, "I sure didn't suspect you had anything to do with that holdup. How did you get involved?"

"Those fellers who held up the bank were friends of mine. They told me their plans and said that if I made a point of being out of town at the time of the robbery, they would give me a fair share of the take. They agreed to hide it under a big log along the trail on which they planned to make their getaway. They were true to their word and left me this roll of bills amounting to $2,300."

After leaving Gunnison, Clark and his prisoner caught the train to Ridgway, where they boarded the stagecoach for Telluride.

This was the beginning of a friendship between Jim Clark and me that I came to value very highly. In spite of his serious faults, Clark had many admirable qualities, which I learned to appreciate as I got to know him.

During the next few years, I often visited Telluride in the line of duty as Sheriff and Deputy U.S. Marshall. Each time I was there I looked up Jim Clark, who lived in an old cabin down along the creek in the willows on the outskirts of town.

Each evening he patrolled the town, and whenever I was there, he insisted upon my accompanying him. He kept strict order in Telluride, and if there were any noisy demonstrations anywhere, he soon put a stop to it.

He was a man of strong character, great courage, and fanatically loyal to his friends. He had a self-made set of standards, which he lived up to, so he was not without principal. He was a capable peace officer and probably did more than any other man to bring law and order to Telluride.

In those days, there was often just a thin line between a lawman and an outlaw. Wyatt Earp, for instance, was a highwayman even while he was Marshall of Tombstone. Wild Bill Hickock was a natural killer and often shot men down for minor offenses without giving them a fair draw. Yet, these lawman and their like, of which I knew many, played a major role in the winning of the West. Their good deeds outshone their bad. So it was with Jim Clark.

One day, sometime later, I received a telegram from Charlie Watson dated August 7, 1895. It read, "Jim Clark killed last night. Come if you can."

When I arrived in Telluride the next evening, Judge Graggert and Charlie Watson met me at the depot. They told me what had happened.

About midnight on August 6, Jim was walking down Main Street toward his cabin with a man known as Mexican Sam. As they passed the Columbia Saloon, a shot rang out in the night. Clark grabbed his chest with hands, exclaiming, "I'm shot, go for the doctor!"

He then turned halfway around and walked into the middle of the street, peering at the roofs of the buildings in that block as if looking for an assassin. Unable to locate him, he returned to the sidewalk and fell in front of Agee's Barbershop.

The bullet had passed downward through one of his lungs and came out beneath his right shoulder blade. The injury might not have been fatal if the slug hadn't severed an artery. As it was, Clark bled to death within fifty minutes.

About everyone in town attended the funeral, including not only the shady element and the many children and needy people who he had befriended, but also the most respected citizens of the community, showing mutual respect for the man who had done so much to bring law and order to Telluride.

That night, after Clark was buried, I went down to his cabin. Tearing up a plank in the floor, I took out his slicker, cap, and false whiskers and burned them. It was the last favor that I could bestow upon a loyal friend, who, like most of us, had a lot of good in him as well as a lot of bad.

Jim Clark's grave is in the Lone Tree Cemetery at Telluride and his epitaph read, "Clark, famed Telluride Marshall, was shot from ambush on August 6, 1895, while passing the Columbia Saloon on Main Street."

One of the most sensational stagecoach holdups in Colorado happened in 1863, when twelve highwaymen held up the Como stage. The take for the outlaws was $80,000 in gold and other valuables. A company of Denver City cavalrymen chased them and finally caught up with them at Palmer Lake, Colorado. Six of the outlaws were killed on the spot, and six others were arrested. The outlaws did not have the loot on them and never confessed where they had left it.

Gold shipped by stagecoach was a well-guarded secret, yet, in spite of such high security, robberies still occurred. No one could figure out how outlaws would know when the gold was being shipped, since only a very few knew the exact time and date that a particular stagecoach line would be carrying the precious gold.

In one instance, officers responsible for thwarting an attempted robbery received a very unwelcome surprise. An outlaw, hiding amid the rocks beside the old stage road,

Photo of an authentic western strong box. Sometimes called a "Treasure Box," as it often held thousands of dollars in gold dust.

Author's Collection

Photo of a diorama depicting a stage hold-up at Ft. Garland

Photo by Author

jumped out in front of the stage in an attempt to hold it up. The law officers shot and killed the outlaw on the spot. News reverberated around the county that, when they took off the bandit's hood, the officers were shocked to find a woman. And not just any woman: She was wife to one of the officers that apprehended her. The lawman couldn't stand the shame of taking her back to town, so she was buried beside the trail where the holdup took place. The gravestone stands today and can easily be seen from Highway 24. The gravestone, though old and worn by the weather and time, reads: "My Wife — Jane Kirkman, Died March 7, 1879. Aged 38 years, 3 months, 7 days."

People caught stealing in Colorado were generally punished in one of three ways. Public horse whipping was punishment for minor offenses. In some cases, the culprit was expelled from the town or area temporarily — and sometimes permanently. The most traditional of all punishments — and the trademark of western justice — was hanging. A hanging was held publicly for robberies, murders, horse stealing, and other felonies.

The Rocky Mountain News, *August 16, 1885*

The Rocky Mountain stage, Mail and Express Line, between Georgetown and Middle Park was robbed last Monday. Six horses and wagons were taken. The suspected thieves were J. H. Colthorp, J. Middleton, and J. V. Thompson, as they were seen leaving with the wagon.

Colthorp was a partner in the Stage Company until quite recently when the company dissolved. Upon dissolution, Colthorp could not agree with J. L. Alexander, the present proprietor of the line, though terms were finally reached and almost entirely settled at the time Colthorp ran away with the stock. His companions, Thompson and Middleton, were formerly drivers on the line. Middleton is the young man who was recently arrested and bound over to appear before the United States Grand Jury for opening and destroying United States Mail belonging to another. The parties were going toward Routt County with the horses and wagons when last seen.

Mr. Alexander has purchased additional horses for the stageline, which is now running on schedule.

CHAPTER SEVEN

EARLY STAGE COMPANIES IN COLORADO

To the joy and delight of the settlers out West, an overland mail service, subsidized by Congress in 1857, was voted to begin as soon as the proper equipment could be acquired. The coaches would run from the Mississippi River to San Francisco. The first step in organizing this service was to allow private industry to acquire horses and coaches for carrying passengers and mail. The route would be traveled in twenty-five days or less, if possible, and was to begin within twelve months after the contract was signed.

In 1858, William Russell developed a new stageline named the Leavenworth & Pike's Peak Express. In 1859, the line was incorporated and was later owned by William Russell and his partners, John Jones and Luther Smoot. The successful completion of this 687-mile journey made the prospectors and the settlers shout with joy. It meant the connection of two widely separated regions.

Two Concord coaches of the Leavenworth and Pike's Peak Express Company left Kansas en route to Denver City, arriving on Saturday, May 7, 1859, and making a dramatic means of new transportation available to the Rocky Mountain West. It brought new hope to settlers who had not received their mail in over a year. This made them feel as if they were no longer isolated on the frontier.

Receipt dated October 6, 1863, Denver City, Colorado Territory, for transport of gold dust. The Overland Stage Line; Ben Holladay, proprietor.

Courtesy of Denver Public Library, Western History Collection.

In 1861, The Leavenworth and Pike's Peak Express sold out to Ben Holladay's Overland Mail and Express Co. Ben Holladay was born in the Kentucky Hills in 1824 and was exposed to wagon trains at an early age. His father managed wagon trains and often traveled through the Cumberland Gap. By the time of the California gold rush era, Ben was an important businessman, owning wagon trains, gold mines in California, and a fleet of steamboats on the Sacramento River.

Ben Holladay became the new owner of the Overland Mail Express in 1862. He began at once to replace horses and coaches on his line. He remodeled all of the old stations and hired new employees, costing him a total of over $2,000,000.

Because the demand was so great to deliver mail and goods to Denver City, he established the "New Overland Trail." Regular mail delivery to Denver City took quite some time, however, as Holladay did not follow through on his promises. The mail was finally delivered three times a week. By spring of 1864, The Overland Mail Express had a monopoly on the route between the Missouri River and the Great Salt Lake. Being the biggest individual employer in the United States, Holladay controlled over 2,670 miles of stageline.

Ben Holladay traveled over his own route twice every year. His private coach was especially built for him with spiral springs and luxurious accessories. He had a mattress for sleeping and a writing desk built in so that he could continue with his business as he traveled. Behind his coach, another one followed, carrying his servants, cooks, and supplies. Six sleek horses pulled his coach, traveling at exceptional speeds.

When Holladay bought out the Butterfield Overland Dispatch in 1866, it became known as the Holladay Overland Mail and Express Company. However, on November 1, 1866, he sold the entire enterprise to the Wells Fargo Company. Ben Holladay lost his fortune in the stock market crash of 1873 and died in Portland, Oregon, on July 8, 1887.

From 1855 until 1861, Russell, Majors, and Waddell were considered to be some of the most influential and substantial businessmen in the West. Their drafts and notes were accepted anywhere, for any amount, in those days. They contributed to the settlement of the Rocky Mountain region by providing transportation, mail, and express facilities, as well as the freighting of essential supplies. More than any businessmen, they were responsible for bridging the gap between the Missouri River and the West.

John Butterfield, a well known stagecoach driver in the East, bid successfully for a six-year contract to begin his own stagelines. He was born in 1801 in New York and had received very little formal education; but Butterfield, who was fifty-six at the time, began working furiously on his new line. He hired employees who were friendly to the Indian tribes — whose land they would travel through day after day. He purchased animals and coaches for his line. He accumulated more than a thousand horses, seven hundred mules, eight hundred sets of harness, and about two hundred and fifty Concord stagecoaches and wagons.

It took an entire year before John could begin his stagecoaching business. His employees worked feverishly at building bridges across streams, removing huge rocks from the trails, and clearing mountain passes.

John Butterfield, who was known by his long, yellow linen duster and flat-brimmed hat, told his drivers, "Remember, boys, that nothing on God's earth must stop the mail!" He began by carrying only four passengers per stage, but, as time wore on, he would carry nine or more.

Butterfield warned his passengers with a large poster that said,

"YOU WILL BE TRAVELING THROUGH
INDIAN COUNTRY AND THE SAFETY
OF YOUR PERSON CANNOT BE
VOUCHSAFED BY ANYONE BUT GOD."

One of John Butterfield's Overland stagecoaches attacked by Indians on the plains in 1866. One of Harper's Weekly's *artists experienced this attack first hand. Butterfield had 250 stagecoaches and wagons, employed 800 men, and kept 1,000 horses and mules busy.*
Courtesy of *Harper's Weekly*, April 23, 1881, Western Reflections Publishing Company Collection

Butterfield's men were tough enough to handle the hardships that his line of work presented them. Congress had awarded Butterfield a $600,000 grant, but, despite this head start, he still owed large debts to the Wells Fargo Company. In March of 1860, John Butterfield turned over the stage route to the Wells Fargo Company.

❧ ❧

One of the most famous stagelines in the West was Wells Fargo & Company. They set out to build the largest stagecoach network in the world. Wells Fargo and Company, in 1868, made the largest single order of Concord coaches ever purchased from Abbot, Downing, and Company in Concord, New Hampshire.

CHAPTER 7: EARLY STAGE COMPANIES

Henry Wells and William Fargo, the two directors of the American Express Company, founded Wells Fargo & Company in the 1860s and, by the end of the century, had over 2,800 branch offices and nearly 38,000 miles of stagecoach lines and express routes. Wells Fargo & Co.'s legendary, colorfully painted, Concord stagecoaches traveled 3,135 miles between California and Nebraska, and north into Montana and Idaho.

Well-known for their red brick buildings with green shutters, Wells Fargo offices were scattered throughout the West. The stagelines continued to grow as they acquired the famous Overland Stage Lines, the Pioneer Overland Stage Lines, and took control of the Butterfield Stageline.

In 1869, Wells Fargo met one of their biggest challenges as they drove their stages through a harsh Rocky Mountain winter. The snow halted all train service, but the Wells Fargo stage came in on time. "The coach due here this afternoon left Cheyenne on time, with two drivers and plenty of shovels," reported *The Rocky Mountain News.*

In the spring of 1867, Wells Fargo announced plans to build an extension of the mountain route from Central City into Georgetown. It was advertised that coaches would leave Denver City and arrive in Georgetown in time for afternoon tea.

When bridges along the route were tested and found to be unsafe, Wells Fargo announced that, when the road was made to be more reliable, they

Wells Fargo Coach loaded with passengers in the mountains.

Courtesy of Wells Fargo and Co.

Wells Fargo and Co. stagecoach with matched Kentucky Horses.
Courtesy of Colorado Historical Society.

would add a line of six-horse coaches. Mountain roads were often relocated because of terrible wear and tear by freight wagons and winter storms and summer flooding.

Wells Fargo & Company kept detailed, precise records of passenger travel in the days of their tenure. From their records, it was indicated that a greater number of men traveled by stagecoach on a frequent basis than did women.

Well Fargo & Company's stagecoaches ran in Colorado Territory from late 1866 until 1869.

❧ ❧

Barlow & Sanderson's stagelines were formed almost at the end of the transcontinental stageline era. By 1870, most of the Southern Overland Mail route was located southwest of Santa Fe. Bradley Barlow and Jared Sanderson knew that their main line along their Colorado mountain branch would be short lived because of the encroachment of the railroads. They planned their southern route through Cañon City, up the Arkansas River, and across the San Luis Valley in 1874. At that time the railroad ended just short of Cañon City.

Barlow and Sanderson originally bought thirty-eight head of "fine American horses" for their stagelines. In the spring of 1875, they bought fifty-two head of horses from St. Louis and six new four-horse Concord coaches to keep up with their business. By then, their route from Cañon City to Del Norte had become very successful.

Another successful route was from Cucharas westward along the Huerfano River by way of the old county seat of Badito, up and over the Sangre de Cristo Pass, and across the San Luis Valley reaching out to the San Juan country. Barlow and Sanderson also established a daily stage service from Cañon City to Rosita, a small mining town in the Wet Mountain Valley.

In late March, time schedules were published between La Veta and Lake City. The time for this trip was thirty-five hours. In March of 1877, General William Jackson Palmer of the Denver and Rio Grande Railroad reported that stagecoaches were carrying fifteen passengers at the rate of eighteen cents per mile.

There is very little known about Bradley Barlow and Jared Sanderson. Their paperwork stated that Kansas City was their principal place of business. However, Barlow continued at his job of cashier of the Vermont National Bank in St. Albans and as the treasurer of Franklin County in 1867. In 1868, he was elected senator of Franklin County, Vermont, and so was rarely seen on the line.

Jared Sanderson was the active manager of the stagelines. The company received many plaudits from satisfied passengers. The *Pueblo Chieftain* ran an article about the Southern Overland Mail with the headline, *"A Model Stageline,"* describing the comfortable coaches and magnificent horses. A passenger returning from Santa Fe was quoted in Denver's *Rocky Mountain News* as saying, among other things:

A Barlow and Sanderson stagecoach from 1873 being shown in a parade at San Luis, Colorado, in July 1951.

Courtesy of Colorado Historical Society

A BUMPY RIDE

The stageline of Barlow and Sanderson and Company cannot be surpassed in the excellence of its appointments. Everything that can be thought of is done for the comfort of the passenger. If one was too warm in crossing the passes, it was because there were too many buffalo robes and blankets piled on us. We were fortunate to have as our drivers, Big Nick and Jack Timmons, to whose tender care we send our friends who have occasion to travel over the road in the future.

The Rocky Mountain News, April 30, 1884, reported,

The J. L. Sanderson and Company stageline, with headquarters in Ouray, has sold their Colorado Stageline to an eastern syndicate, who will take immediate possession.

※ ※

In 1873, about the time placer mining began along the Arkansas River and along California Gulch, Bob Spottswood and William McClelland began operating a stage and express line. Their route came from Colorado Springs to Cañon City by way of the Arkansas River to Granite and Oro. It would be five years before the discovery of great lead and silver deposits that made Leadville famous.

When the U.S. Post Office found out about the Leadville discoveries, the government advertised for bids for a stageline to carry the mail from Denver City and leave for Leadville on a daily basis. Bob Spottswood traveled to Washington and secured the contract. The establishment of this line meant spending great sums of money on horses and coaches; however, these men apparently had abundant capital, and the line was soon in business.

McClelland and Spottswood routed their stagelines through many mining towns. They began in Denver City, then went west to Morrison, and up through what is now Turkey Creek Canyon to Fairplay.

Bob Spottswood recognized the importance of the silver discoveries and soon developed a stageline that ran from Fairplay over the narrow and breathtaking Weston Pass into Leadville. This line, though harrowing, saved forty miles through the much lower Trout Creek Pass.

When Leadville was booming, there was more than one stagecoach line vying for business. Besides Spottswood and McClelland, Barlow and Sanderson and Wall and Witter were also competing for passengers and express. When the Rio Grande Railroad and its various other branches reached the mining areas of the Colorado Rockies, Bob Spottswood and

Billy McClelland sold their stagelines, stock, and equipment to the firm of Barlow and Sanderson. They were some of the few stageline owners that retired as wealthy men. Bob Spottswood remained a well-respected Colorado citizen until the time of his death in 1910.

In addition to the many large, well-known stage companies in Colorado, there were dozens of small stageline companies in existence in the late 1800s. It seemed that there was a stageline for every small town and community in Colorado. When the railroads encroached on the business of the major stagelines, smaller lines continued to operate by picking up and delivering passengers to places not yet reachable by train.

Hockaday and Hall, 1854-1858, had a line from St. Joseph, Missouri, to Salt Lake City along a portion of the Oregon Trail. Missouri Stage Company established an express and passenger connection up the Arkansas River to Cañon City, Tarryall, Old Colorado City, and Denver City. The W.L. Smith Stageline served Caribou and Nederland from Boulder and from Central City and Black Hawk. Cottrill, Vickroy and Company's first direct mail coach from Bent's Old Fort reached Denver City on September 28, 1862.

The Circle Route Stageline was the main transportation between Montrose, Ouray, and Silverton. At least four stages left daily from Lott's Hotel and the D. & R. G. Express. The Colorado Stage Company operated in 1870 between

The old Circle Route Stage being shown in the Pioneers Parade in 1922, Montrose, Colorado. Western Slope Fair, 1922.

Courtesy of Colorado Historical Society

Circle Route
advertisement
1907.
Courtesy of
Ouray County
Historical
Museum

the towns of Black Hawk, Central City, Denver, Georgetown, Golden City, and Idaho Springs. Dave Wood, who also owned a very successful freighting company, owned the San Juan Stageline. He called his route, "The Magnolia Route," and it ran all over the San Juan mountain country.

The Denver, Santa Fe, and Express Company was owned by Abraham Jacobs and William Jones. It began July 28, 1867, between Denver City and Trinidad. Western Stage Company was one of the first of the larger organizations to operate into the mountains beyond Golden City. In 1860, the Western Stage Company had a line from Denver City to Old Colorado City. Hinckley and Company's Mountain Express first began to haul gold dust from the mountains in June of 1860, transporting it to the newly established mint of Clark, Gruber and Company of Denver City.

The Kehler and Montgomery Express Company began to tap the express business in 1859. The Express Company extended a line from Denver City to Golden City, through the Golden Gate to Gregory's Diggings and Mountain City. The Mt. Vernon Express created quite a lot of excitement among miners when it first appeared in Mountain City. The first coach, driven by Billy Updike, pulled into the central mountain town amid cheering from the miners.

Reich and Hanson Stagelines was the first stage to run back and forth between Paonia, Hotchkiss, and Delta. It was established by Joseph Reich and Ed Hanson in the 1880s to haul freight express and passengers. Meserole and Blake Stagelines ran from Rico to Ophir in 1879. Denver & Steamboat Springs Stage Company ran a line between Denver, Granby, Hot Sulphur Springs, Kremmling, Steamboat Springs, and Craig. S.W. Nott Stage Company ran a line over the "high line" over Loveland Pass H.R. Hammond ran a stageline from Gunnison to Delta and Grand Junction. D.F. Watson's

Stageline ran from Silverton to Telluride. John Prowers ran a stageline near Las Animas and Boggsville. In addition to these, there were many others, such as The Kansas City Gold Hunter's Express Transportation Company, The Pike's Peak Express, and Whipple and Stafford in 1888.

Entrepreneurship and free enterprise were alive and well in Colorado in the 1800s. Some stagelines and their owners lasted only a few years — if that

This stagecoach was probably part of the "Circle Route," a thousand mile trip which began in Denver on the Denver and Rio Grande Railroad. Before the Rio Grande Southern Railroad was finished in 1892, the Circle Route trip was made to Ouray by train and then by stagecoach from Ouray to Red Mountain or Silverton where the trip continued by railroad. Even after the RGS was built, there were many travelers who preferred to take the stagecoach trip because of the unforgettable beauty of the route and the total uniqueness of the stagecoach trip, which was a form of transportation that had virtually disappeared in the United States after the advent of the train. This particular stage has at least eight passengers, six up on top and two peering through the windows. There may be more passengers inside. The man on top carries a rifle, probably more for sport and certainly not for needed protection. It is likely that at least a few of the passengers are tourists on the Circle Route, since some 10,000 of them came through Ouray each summer during this time.

Courtesy of Western Reflections Publishing Company Collection

— and changed owners regularly. The editor of the *Kansas City Daily Journal of Commerce* reported that, "The glory of stagecoaches is passing away, and the locomotive with its train will soon bear our merchandise westward."

The Rocky Mountain News, *May 9, 1859:*

This is the beginning of a stupendous enterprise undertaken by the above named express company, Leavenworth and Pike's Peak Express. By the energy of this company, a new route is marked out for the immigrants across the plains; one that can be followed without the risk of starvation and lingering death.

Stations are being established at intervals of 25 miles after leaving Junction City. It crosses the Beaver, Bijou, and Kiowa Creeks, tributaries of the Platte, and passes through beautiful pine country for 60 miles. It strikes Cherry Creek twenty miles above its mouth. The road throughout its whole length is good, when broken and traveled, but the coaches that have just arrived made the first track over it.

CHAPTER EIGHT

HARDSHIPS ON THE TRAIL

There was a certain ritual undergone when a stagecoach was loading passengers, mail, express, or otherwise preparing to embark on the next leg of its journey. The team was impatient as the coach was loading. They were snorting, stamping their feet, and swishing their tails — all in an effort to get the show on the road. The treasure box, usually made of iron and lead, was loaded into the front boot under the driver's feet. This box contained the most valuable items, such as payroll, gold dust, and passengers' valuables.

At the back of the coach was another boot where passengers' baggage, lumpy bags of printed matter, and express packages were stowed. The nine passengers who had just eaten their breakfast filed out of the hotel and took their seats in the coach, which would be their home for several days to come. Some passengers broke out a deck of cards to play a hand of poker. Others told stories, became acquainted with each other, and talked about the weather.

One of the most unpleasant features of stagecoaching was the dust. In the mountains, there was also the continual bouncing and jolting of the coach as the team ran at full gallop down the scariest roads and over huge outcroppings of rock. When traveling in the Rocky Mountains, passengers recalled rounding a steep mountain curve. "We found nothing but blue sky. We literally flew around those steep curves swinging over the abyss and then swinging back easily toward the bank. In some places we couldn't see the lead horses around the curve." They were probably not in as much danger as they suspected because the driver had complete control of his team. He would have known his team's limitations and could speak to them with expert flicks of the ribbons.

On a long trip, the time would eventually come when the passengers would be hoping for it to end. Where passengers were confined to such a small space as a stagecoach cabin, there would often be angry words exchanged with each other. In March, 1866, a passenger on the Overland Route went berserk, stabbed a fellow passenger, and then killed a second passenger with the pistol he was carrying, wounding a third man in the process before being killed himself — all within the confines of the coach.

In *From the Atlantic to the Pacific Overland*, published in 1866, Demas Barnes wrote:

> *The condition of one man's running stages to make money, while another seeks to ride for pleasure, are not in harmony to provide comfort. Coaches will be overloaded, passengers will get sick, a polite gentleman will offer to hold the screaming baby, children will cry, passengers get angry, the drivers will swear, the sensitive will shrink, and the dirt is almost unbearable. Stop overnight? No, you wouldn't! To sleep on the dirt of a one-story sod or adobe hut, without a chance to wash up, with miserable food, uncongenial companionship, loss of seat in the coach until one becomes empty, won't work. A through ticket and fifteen inches of space to sit, with a fat man on one side, and a poor widow on the other, a baby on your lap, a hatbox over your head and three or four passengers immediately in front, leaning against your knees, makes the picture, as well as your sleeping space for the trip. I have just finished six days and nights of this very thing, and I am free to say, until I forget a great many things now very visible to me, I shall never ever, undertake it again..*

Besides the deplorable conditions that many passengers had to endure, accidents also occasionally occurred. The *Rocky Mountain News* noted several stagecoach mishaps in 1861. One such item read, "Gregory coach was again overturned descending Smith Hill. No one was seriously hurt." Once in a while a serious accident occurred, such as the one on a steep grade at Kenyon's Mill. The Denver to Central City coach was descending the steep grade and, instead of making the curve, it went straight ahead and ended up on the bottom of the ravine. Nine people escaped with minor injuries, although the driver was seriously hurt.

Roads were often in such bad condition due to weather or poor construction that accidents were practically bound to happen. There were many trips where only the driver's extreme skill in controlling his team made it possible to have a safe journey.

One morning in 1893, a stage driver named Chauncey Mills left Ouray and headed for the Revenue Mine at the town of Sneffels. Mills, who drove both stagecoaches and freight teams, had just reached Windy Point when one of his horses went off the side of the road. While he and his helpers tried to get the horse safely back up onto the embankment, an avalanche broke loose and swept the entire outfit down the side of the mountain. Two of Mills' men were killed, but Mills grabbed onto a tree and was rescued.

This photo is of a young Chauncey Mills who often drove stagecoaches. He survived an avalanche southwest of Ouray in 1893.

Courtesy of Bud Mills, Montrose, Colorado, and the Mills Family

A BUMPY RIDE

Near Colorado Springs on July 28, 1899, a young man in charge of the stagecoach was proceeding toward the city. He had some experience in driving a stagecoach, but not quite enough to prevent an accident from happening. The stage left Cripple Creek at nine o'clock in the morning and was due in Colorado Springs at 3:30 p.m. While maneuvering the team around a sharp curve, he met a wagon coming uphill in his path. The road, badly rutted from frequent mountain rains, was difficult to drive over; and, while he tried to pull his horses over to let the wagon pass, the coach and team hit a big rut and toppled over on its side, scattering passengers all over the road. To say the coach was overloaded would be an understatement. There were twenty-three passengers riding on a coach made to hold nine. Many hung onto the sides of the coach or sat up on top of it, while the inside of the coach was so full of people that it was nearly bursting at the seams.

When the stagecoach toppled over, the coach, as one of the functions of its design, allowed the horses to become free. The horses, wild with panic and fear, began to run down the mountain, dragging part of the harness (a broken single tree). Two of the horses were badly injured before the driver could bring them under control. One of the horses died on the spot from injuries incurred, and a second one had to be destroyed. The passengers were not badly injured, but many of them walked the rest of the way to the Broadmoor Hotel, where they received medical attention.

In July of 1877, a writer, Henry Williams, reported an accident just outside of Del Norte. Mr. Williams wrote the *Williams Tourist Guide*, which was very popular at the time. He was a passenger on a heavily loaded coach thirty miles from Del Norte, when the wheels hit an oversized rut in the road. When the driver was thrown from the coach, the horses realized that they had free rein and began to gallop toward the next stage stop.

As the stage careened down the road at a high rate of speed, some of the passengers decided to jump from the coach rather than wait for the inevitable crash. When the horses reached the station, they were still moving at a full gallop. As they approached the gatepost, the coach broadsided it and overturned.

There were thirteen people riding on the coach that day, and, by sheer luck, no one was killed in the wreck. Mr. Williams, however, suffered a broken left ankle, leaving him partially crippled for the rest of his life.

Varmints and other pests were also a danger or aggravation to stagecoach passengers. As a result, many of the passengers carried guns. Frank A. Root, a mail agent at Latham Station in Colorado in the 1800s, said that occasionally passengers would pull out their pistols and shoot at herds of antelope only a few hundred yards from their coach. They also enjoyed the sport of shooting at coyotes and jackrabbits, but were rarely successful in bringing one down.

Root reported that, along the Platte in 1863 and 1864, he shot quite a number of rattlesnakes from the stage. Rattlesnakes were numerous on the plains in those days.

One coach coming in from the west informed Latham Station that there were swarms of grasshoppers migrating in the direction of the station. A few days later, a horde of red-legged locusts descended upon them like an avalanche. The locusts landed all over the area and ate every blade of grass, shrub, and weed. They were so numerous that they darkened the sky as they flew in.

Some annoying pests in those days that nearly drove people crazy were lice, bedbugs, and fleas. Many of the passengers carried them on the stage. Some men were fairly covered with them. It was probably due to the fact that their mattresses were filled with hay and were infested with them, and their blankets were also seldom washed. During the winter season, the company employees rarely bathed, and the pests became even more troublesome.

One pest that bothered the stock and the employees of the stagelines was called a "Buffalo Gnat." They were so tiny that they could not be seen with the naked eye, but they could be felt — especially when they would bite you behind the ears. They were annoying, and nothing seemed to discourage them from taking up residence on one's skin. They could pretty near torment the life out of any animal or human being.

Fall and winter travel became almost a necessity for avoiding swarms of mosquitoes. In low-lying areas along creeks and places where wood and water were available, clouds of mosquitoes tormented humans. Black gnats and mosquitoes attacked in swarms, and chiggers and wood ticks were a daily, early-summer nuisance.

The most dangerous hazard to early day stagecoach travelers was human — angry Indians attacked the stagecoach on a regular basis. The Indians claimed that the white settlers had invaded their land and endangered their hunting grounds. They complained that hunters slaughtered off the buffalo and other game indiscriminately. All of their complaints were valid, but no one was listening; in fact, the United States Government was accused of breaking treaty after treaty and failing to keep their promises. In 1862 and 1863, Plains Indians acquired horses and firearms from attacks on wagon trains and stagecoaches, even though troops were stationed along the different routes.

In September of 1863, Governor Evans of Colorado kept in contact with traders who knew what was going on in the Indian communities.

He arranged to meet with some of the Indians north of Denver City to make yet another peace treaty. Unfortunately, not many Indians came to the meeting, and those that did were stubborn and insolent. As a result, Governor Evans' attempts at peace were a failure.

The postmaster in Denver City complained that the mail service was being interrupted by Indian attacks. Latham Station, at one point, had about three tons of sacked mail, which they used to pile up against the windows for extra protection against attack. Horses and provisions continued to be stolen from the Overland Mail Company, and stations were also destroyed in an effort to stop the mail coaches, which were known to the Indians as "paper wagons."

In 1864, the Overland Stage route was continually under attack, resulting in the deaths of many settlers and emigrants. They lost hundreds of horses and mules, and tons of hay were set on fire and destroyed. Seventy-five miles of wagon roads were ruined, and the telegraph lines were pulled down repeatedly.

Ben Holladay found it difficult to keep enough horses and mules alive and healthy on the Overland Routes to run his stagecoaches. Finally in 1866 the Civil War ended, and the United States Government began to receive peace overtures from tribes of Sioux and Cheyenne. Also in that year, a peace council began at Fort Laramie with representatives from the U.S. Government and the hostile Indian tribes in attendance.

Some Indian tribes refused to honor the peace treaties, however, so violence and bloodshed continued across the plains. The Indian problems finally decreased when more military stockades were built along the stage routes. The Indian tribes had cause to be outraged, as miners and immigrants continued to cross the prairie and destroy buffalo and other game, leaving many tribes without adequate food and shelter. It was generally agreed that the government efforts to "civilize" or destroy the Indians had been a dismal failure.

From the old Denver City publication, *Field and Farm*, the following frontier sketches of Indian attacks appeared on July 27, 1907:

> *During the summers of 1866 and 1867, the number of passengers and drivers killed en route was nearly 200. Those were the two most serious years in the history of overland travel. Along the routes which crossed Western Kansas, Nebraska, and Eastern Colorado, the Indians would lie in ambush near where they knew it was customary for the stages to stop for water and for some other necessary purpose and there they would make their attacks, firing at the passengers and drivers and circling around at a rapid gallop*

making a most uncertain target for the aim of the travelers. One of the most noteworthy of these incidents was the ambush at Plum Creek on the old Platte River Trail.

The overland coach always stopped at the Plum Creek station for half an hour or so to water and rest the horses and give the passengers the freedom of a few moments exercise away from the cramped quarters inside the coach. Of this habitual pause the Indians must have known for they attacked the coach, killed the driver and all the passengers with the exception of a little girl who had wandered away up the creek to gather some sand plums. After the Indians left, the girl wandered along the trail and sighted a wagon train led by Alexander Majors.

The wagon train could not conveniently take the little girl along as no provision had been made for passengers, so Majors called for a volunteer to return her to Atchison, Kansas. Buffalo Bill Cody happened to be along with the wagon train and valiantly tendered his services. He took an extra horse and escorted the girl safely across the plains. After the duty was performed, he immediately left Atchison and rode along the Platte River alone for several days and finally overtook the Majors outfit before they reached Denver City. There were many attacks made on the stages in the 1860s, attacks that make interesting reading now, although they were terrifying at the time, but the most notable was that one at Plum Creek in which Buffalo Bill came into the limelight.

Serious disease and illness was another hardship on long stagecoach journeys. There was very little medicine available along the stage routes at that time; and, for the most part, what was available was not adequate to effectively treat the passengers.

Some of the dreaded diseases of the period were typhoid fever, dysentery, diarrhea, and cholera. Some passengers carried quinine in case something bad would afflict them or their family. It was a terrible hardship to be sick while on the trail.

Typhoid fever was a very serious disease among those who traveled the Santa Fe Trail. Travelers were forced to drink water wherever they could find it, even if the water was unclean. It was common at the time for travelers to camp around a spring where others had camped before them. The springs and water holes were usually set in a low spot of land where human and animal waste would eventually drain into them. Since drinking unclean water generally caused the disease, many people died as a result.

Often the services of a physician were needed on the overland route, but, up until the early part of 1863, there was not a doctor on the plains between Fort Kearney and Denver City — a distance of 400 miles. Now and then it was necessary to go 200 miles for a physician. During the spring of 1863, Doctor Lewis, hailing from Ohio, relocated on the South Platte between Alkali Lake and old Julesburg. Soon he fell into the good graces of the Indians. He was not there very long, however, before he married a young squaw, took up his permanent residence in one of their tepees, and was seldom available to white travelers.

The success and pleasure involved in traveling a trail often depended upon the weather, which was often considered to be the major hardship of a trip. Eastern Colorado was often hot and dry, and the dust created by the horse teams and the running gear often sifted into the coach, making it almost impossible for the people sitting inside to breathe. If there was a thunderstorm or windstorm, which were frequent on the plains, the coach's canvas curtains would have to be pulled down, making for very little ventilation; and, if snow or heavy rain caused the coach to become stuck, passengers would often be forced to aid the driver in freeing it.

Frank A. Root recalled, "Along the Platte River, where the wagon traffic and livestock traffic was the greatest, there were clouds of dust, sometimes lasting for two or three days. The best cure for the problem was to wear a veil or bandana so one could cover up most of their face."

The worst snowstorm Colorado had seen for over twenty years happened in January 1865. Ab Williamson, the coach driver, left Middle Boulder in Colorado Territory at about 4:00 p.m. on a threatening January afternoon. The passengers included an army officer from Fort Laramie, a merchant from Atchison and his teenage daughter, two miners, and a Holladay mule buyer. Not long after leaving Boulder, the weather grew perilous. Snow was beginning to fall heavily, and vision was nearly impossible. Williamson encouraged his team to keep going, accidentally heading them into a huge snowdrift, where they became stuck. For supper, the passengers had to share the driver's lunch and a couple of sandwiches the girl had brought with her. The driver also had a bottle of wine, which he shared with all of the passengers. The miners and the army officer volunteered to seek help. When they reached St. Vrain, they spread the news of their snowbound stage, and a group of men was sent immediately to help rescue them. By the time the rescue crew reached the stage, the passengers had been there for two days and nights. No serious injuries were incurred.

In early November 1862, the eastbound mail coach to Denver was delayed for two days because of a raging storm, which resulted in high

An Overland Mail Coach crossing the Rocky Mounains in a snow storm. This illustration was published early in 1868. The Butterfield stages were still in use at this time, carrying passengers and mail.
Courtesy of *Harper's Weekly*, February 8, 1868. Western Reflections Publishing Company Collection

water. It was later reported that the storm was the most destructive one to occur in many years in terms of the death of animals and other livestock.

On Raton Pass, about two months after the preceding high water incident, a coach skidded on a patch of ice and fell dozens of feet down an embankment, where it rolled completely over twice. The passengers were not badly hurt even though the stage was overloaded, but the coach was badly damaged.

Winter dangers were very real in the San Juan Mountains. Warm days and cold nights caused huge icicles to form on the overhanging cliffs above Camp Bird Mine. If one hit a man or animal it would easily kill them. The San Juans record the most avalanches in the state almost every year. The

Waterhole Slide took the lives of four travelers and sixteen horses in the winter of 1909. Miners frequently purposely caused slides with gunshots in order to control when they came down.

Heavy downpours of rain could often cause as much or more damage to stagecoaches as snow. Often times, stagecoaches came to a standstill waiting for water to subside before the driver could safely cross a raging stream. Even at that, passengers were still willing to take the risk of traveling by stagecoach, knowing that it might involve wet clothing and long delays.

Flash floods were a constant concern in the summer, especially in steep mountain canyons. Since many of the roads used by travelers were actually creek beds, it didn't take much for a rainstorm to endanger the lives of the passengers on a stagecoach. The steep mountains became like a funnel, accumulating large amounts of water in the valleys and arroyos between.

When the trip finally came to a close, the passengers would seek out a hotel where they could have a bath and a real bed to sleep on. The travelers were relieved that the long trip was over, but they took pride in the fact that they had braved such dangers and participated in an unforgettable adventure.

The Ouray Herald, *April 24, 1903*

The stage from Red Mountain, Tuesday, driven by Clint Buskirk, was abandoned this side of Ironton on account of the horrible condition of the road, and the mail bags were brought down on a horse. The loose snow along the roadside is 7 to 10 feet deep, and the well-beaten path in the roadway had become soft and sloppy and the horses were unable to walk in them, breaking through the sides. One horse fell down so often that he finally refused to get up, and the driver shoveled the snow away from him so he could lie on bare ground and left him there until the next morning. He went back up and brought him and the stage down while the snow was still frozen. The mail will now be carried on a packhorse until the snow is melted.

CHAPTER NINE

PASSENGER MEMOIRS OF THE STAGECOACH ERA

he following memoirs remind us that keeping a journal is an effective and wonderful way to record what will eventually become our history:

❧ DEMAS BARNES ❧

Denver, Colorado Territory, June 21, 1865

I had not deemed it a great undertaking for another to cross the continent overland, but when I sit here midway, at the foot of the Rocky Mountains, the habits of my life changed — all connection with the accumulated interests of many years of toil suspended, social ties sundered, kind friends and loved ones far behind me, with rugged hills, parched deserts, and lonely wastes far, far ahead, I do feel it is a great undertaking for me — for anyone. Many friends said they envied my trip, would they like to go. I do not doubt their sincerity — I have thought so myself — but I beg to undeceive them. It is not a pleasant, but an interesting trip.

Denver, June 25, 1865

The Indians have interfered with the running of the stages west of here, and it is uncertain when I shall be able to proceed. I have visited the mines in the mountains at Central City and Black Hawk, and returned here to wait my chances....

It was near evening of our second day, calm, delightful, but hot. I was sitting with the driver outside the stage, holding an umbrella to protect me from the tropical heat while in but a linen coat. A cloud appeared in the southeast, a sudden and intensely cold breeze struck us, and I will venture to say the thermometer sank thirty degrees in ten minutes; the whole heavens were streaked with forked lightening; the wind rose to a hurricane that seemed about to snap and rip the very sod from the earth, while as to rain, it might have rained harder before, and it might have rained harder since, but I didn't happen to be out in it. A ship might as well proceed under full sail in a typhoon, as a stage across the plains in one of these storms. Stages are frequently capsized. When occurring in the nighttime, as did one of ours, and which is more usually the case, one is strongly reminded that home would be a very comfortable place to be.

Denver, Colorado, June 26, 1865

It was eight o'clock in the morning, a whip-cracked, a heavy Concord Stage wheeled in front of the office; on it was painted, "Overland." Childish though it might have been, I felt sad; it was a long distance. I was running from letters, from home, from friends. Life is not so full of pleasure that we can afford to put three thousand miles between us and our dearest heart treasures and not feel irresolute and pained. Our effects were soon loaded; 1600 pounds of mail in the boot, our baggage on top exposed to the storm.

Denver, Colorado, June 27, 1865

Denver is a square, prompt little place, which like Pompeii's Pillar, is surrounded by immensity. It is better built than St. Joseph or Atchison, has fine brick stores, four churches, a good seminary, two theatres, two banks, plenty of gambling shops, a fine United States Mint, which I observed had nothing to do, and which had coined the vast amount of forty thousand dollars in a whole year.

Our baggage went under water in fording Boulder Creek, and I am now trying to dry my shirts in the sun, while writing this on my valise, by the side of a hut, surrounded by a dozen or so of my disappointed traveling companions.

CHAPTER 9: PASSENGER MEMOIRS

🌿 SISTER BLANDINA SEGALE 🌿

In 1872, Sister Blandina Segale received word that she had been assigned as a teacher to a mission post at Trinidad, Colorado. She took the train to Kit Carson, Colorado, just west of the Kansas boundary. From this point, she continued on to her destination by stagecoach, traveling the route of the old Santa Fe Trail. Thus began Sister Blandina's twenty-one year career of service in the far Southwest.

> *Trinidad, December 10, 1872*
>
> *My dearest dear: Here I am safe in Trinidad, Colorado Territory, instead of on the Island of Cuba, where we thought I was to go. No wonder this small pebble (Trinidad) is not on our maps.*
>
> *In Kit Carson I ordered the stage for the morning of the 9th. Mrs. Mullen was very attentive. She had new clean hay put in the stage to keep my feet warm, and after I got in she wrapped a large comforter around me, remarking that, "traveling on the plains and in winter is not a pleasant prospect." The driver must have had strict instructions from Otero and Seller, they own the stageline. For the first time I had indefinable fears.*
>
> *At noon the driver came to the stage door and said, "We take dinner here." I thanked him and said, "I do not wish any dinner."*
>
> *"But, lady, we will not have another stopping place to eat until six o'clock this evening." I thanked him again and said, "But I do not wish any dinner." The jolting of the stage and my thoughts had taken all appetite away. Though I could see nothing from the stage, it seemed that the driver aimed to drive over every stone and make the wheels go into every rut. It was nothing but a jerk, up and down, all the way in a stage that had no springs and traveling at the rate of twelve miles an hour.*
>
> *Dear Sister Justina,*
>
> *In a stage built for four passengers, and in which six could be seated by crowding, eight had to ride. Two gentlemen managed, with the aid of two small boxes, to sit between the passengers of front and rear seats of the stage by leaning back to back, hanging their legs outside of the stage door. When this position could no longer be endured, the other two gentlemen passengers relieved them. Those seated suffered greatly from overcrowding, and all endured great heat and thirst. All these tortures combined were in*

a great measure lost sight of in the constant fear of being attacked by Indians.

For the luxury, twenty-five cents a mile was paid, with an allowance of forty pounds of baggage. We made a stop in Denver, going directly to the Planter's Hotel. The Rt. Rev. J. P. Machebeuf was soon informed of our arrival, and he sent his best carriage to have us conveyed to the Convent of the Sisters of Loretto, where, through the kindness of the Sisters, we soon forgot our past fatigues, and made preparations to continue our route to our destination. The stage from Denver to Santa Fe had no occupants but the sisters. This was one comfort, but the fear of Indians kept us in misery.

(FROM THE BOOK, THE OVERLAND TRAIL TO CALIFORNIA, BY FRANK A. ROOT AND WILLIAM ELSEY CONNELLEY)

January 18, 1863

While clerking in the Atchison postoffice, holding the position of assistant postmaster, I was appointed express messenger on the great overland stageline. The "run" was from Atchison, Kansas to Denver City, Colorado, a distance of 653 miles. I was to start on my first trip the following Monday morning, January 23. Although for some time I had had a desire for such a position, the appointment was a complete surprise, and I hardly knew what to think of it.

I was aware that the messenger on the "Overland"' was expected to ride outside, on the box with the driver, and go six days and nights without undressing. I knew that there were also dangers connected with the position; exposure to all kinds of weather, occasional robberies by highwaymen, and assaults from the hostile Indians scattered on the plains along the line. The stage authorities must have a man without delay. To take such a position in warm weather would have been more pleasant, but there happened to be a vacancy at this particular time and it had to be filled.

I went to headquarters and accepted the appointment. With less than five days for preparation, I made every hour count until the date of my departure. Besides my every day wearing apparel, my outfit consisted of a gum coat, a buffalo robe, a pair of blankets, government blue overcoat with a cape, suitable for roughing it on the plains, a pair of flannel overalls, fur muffler, a small shawl, buffalo overshoes, and last but not least, a Wesson Breech-loading rifle, a Colts navy revolver, with belt and scabbard and plenty of ammunition.

My outfit being all arranged, on the following morning I was ready for duty. Repairing to the company's office on Commercial Street, I began to check up on the way-bill for the various packages placed in my charge, a number of them containing treasure, and at eight o'clock, with the valuables in the strongbox, and the box placed in the front boot of the stagecoach, with the bulky packages secure in the rear boot, I buckled on my "hip howitzer" and was prepared for my first trip to Denver.

While making this trip to Denver, I must own up that I was frightened the second night out from Atchison. I did not know, when I first started out, that it was the custom of the drivers, when approaching a station at night, to most always send up a terrible yell. This was done to awaken the stock tender, so he might have the team harnessed, and also that the driver might be ready who was to succeed the incoming one on the next drive. While asleep down in the front boot, under the driver's feet, I was suddenly awakened by what seemed to me one of the most unearthly yells I had ever heard from any human being. It appeared like the horrible yell of an Indian on the warpath. I felt sure that the Indians were after someone's scalp.

It is a pleasure to look back on Colorado as it was a third of a century ago, and note some of the wonderful changes that have taken place during that time. Although some of the days spent on the South Platte at Latham Station in 1863 and 1864 were extremely lonesome, days of great anxiety, still many of them I shall always remember, to cherish among the pleasantest days of my recollection.

🌿 RALPH MOODY (FROM <u>FIRST MAIL WEST</u>) 🌿

This excerpt was recorded on a trip with the first mail on the Santa Fe Stageline from Denver to Bent's Old Fort.

Denver, January 3, 1866
The coach had arrived at Franktown for the midday meal and the passengers had supper at Old Colorado City. The run had taken ten hours for a distance of seventy-five miles, which was thought

to be "pretty good staging." Cold weather prevailed, and snow was deep on the summit of the divide. After the supper stop, travel resumed through the snow, and the Fontaine qui Bouille (Fountain) was reached by daybreak. There was no great rush on the trip from Pueblo because the coach from Santa Fe was expected to be late by half a day or more in reaching Bent's Old Fort. Snow lay on the ground for thirty or forty miles down the Arkansas and then disappeared until about fifteen or twenty miles from the trading post.

I was impressed by the number of irrigated farms along the river below Pueblo, but there still seemed to be an unlimited supply of good land that was still covered with greasewood and sagebrush. About ten miles below Booneville at the stage station near the former Civil War Camp Fillmore, I was annoyed to see about 1,500 tons of hay put up for the government, but no government animals to eat it. Many buffalo had come into the valley of the Arkansas near Spring Bottom, another stage station about twenty miles above Bent's Fort, where hunters were killing them for their bones, hearts and tongues.

The coach finally arrived at Bent's Old Fort a little before 10 a.m.; the one from Santa Fe had come in five hours earlier. The Stage Company had converted the fort into a very complete and comfortable station. I had nothing but praise for the messenger, Arthur Hill, who had charge of the coach from Denver.

🌿 FROM ERNST KOHLBERG'S DIARY: 🌿

A Jewish immigrant named Ernst Kohlberg was making his way from Hamburg, Germany, to El Paso, Texas:

We left Las Animas at 6 a.m., September 27, in a fairly comfortable stagecoach whose motive power was four mules. The coaches are as light and strong as can be built. The sides are gray canvas and heavy leather straps carry the body of the coach, as regular iron and steel springs could snap on the rough roads. Our first day's journey in the coach was over the prairie and the road being fair the trip was quite comfortable.

We reached the Raton Mountains that night and our way led through these mountains to Santa Fe. I am sure I will never forget this ride. We stopped three times daily for twenty minutes for our meals. We also had to stop at intervals for five minutes to change *mules. We traveled day and night and always at a gallop whether the road was good and level or rough, over rocks, up hill and down always at the same gait. Several times I was hurled from my seat and bumped the ceiling of the coach when we hit a real hard bump or went through an arroyo.*

Some ride, It was very hot during the day, while at night it turned real cold. It did not seem to bother the stage driver if he upset the coach, which happened several times. Mr. and Mrs. Schutz and I were turned upside down, but no one was hurt for the coach proper remained lying on its side while the mules went off with the front end. When we finally arrived at Santa Fe, I was happier than I had been when I arrived in New York just a month before.

❧ ABNER E. SPRAGUE, "MY LAST RIDE" ❧

Abner Sprague first settled in Moraine Park, Colorado. Joining him at the Moraine Park homestead were his parents, Thomas and Mary Sprague, who had homesteaded near Loveland. Abner Sprague and his brother, Fred, were partners in a stageline that connected Estes Park and the plains.

Those old days of four and six horse drawn stages are still remembered by many, without doubt, bring back prickles along the spine when they recall the wild stories of the driver, with a

One of Estes Park's earliest pioneers, Abner Sprague, moved into the upper end of Moraine Park, one of the most beautiful valleys in Rocky Mountain National Park, in 1875 and his family homesteaded almost the entire valley. The business was so successful that by 1895 Sprague's hotel, a three story log structure, was written up in guide books. The ranch was sold to the U.S. Government in 1962, and the buildings removed in 1964.

Courtesy of Denver Public Library, Western History Collection

flourish of his long whip, would cause the leaders to lunge toward the edge of the road as though they were going over into the rushing water of the stream down a mountainside.

It was no tame thrill, even if the driver did not try to scare you to death with his expert driving. But mostly, it brings back to the traveler the taste and smell of dust, dust in your eyes, dust in your mouth, dust in your lungs, up your nose and all through your baggage, along with your body being gritty with it from head to toe.

My last trip by stage was from Loveland over the canyon road, which at that time was narrow and rough. The Johnson Brothers, George and B. B. were owners of the stageline when that trip was made during the high water in June the last year the "horse-drawn" was operated. Our driver was George W. Johnson. Among the passengers were two lively girls on the front seat with the driver. Inside were Dr. and Mrs. Wood, bound for Elkhorn Lodge, Mrs. Sprague and myself, and others to fill the rig.

We met the down stage in the foothills and were advised to turn back as the water was over the road in many places and washing badly. Mr. Johnson wanted to turn back when we could find no roadbed to travel over. Water was over the road in many places in the Big Thompson Canyon, but the first place to cause a halt was in Louie Canyon. There, the water was raging through from wall to wall with no sign of a roadbed, but a bend in the stream threw the fierce water away from the roadside. So through we went, Johnson keeping a sharp lookout for any swirl that might indicate a washout.

Nothing was left of the roadbed but the large rocks, the fine material having been washed away. The driver had the lines to hang onto, but those two girls had nothing but each other and the high seat when the stage swayed and bumped over the rocks. When the near lead horse stepped into the high water, he slipped on the sloping rock and went down, the water dashing over him. If only the expression on those girls faces could have been shown.

The driver held the team to the road. The leader recovered his feet at once and they came on through. The girls looked a little dizzy and a little bit seasick, that is their smiles looked a little sickly. Inside, all was well, as we had something to hold onto with both hands.

JOHN B. ARMOR (FROM PIONEER EXPERIENCES IN COLORADO)

I came to Colorado in 1863, when I was eight years old. Our family had been living on a farm six miles west of Atchison,

Kansas, when father decided to move us farther west. He had gone to Colorado in 1859, helping to locate the stations for Russell, Majors and Waddell's Stageline. Then he had to put up a stamp mill on Clear Creek just below Black Hawk.

We traveled the Platte River route. On the way we met no buffaloes and the Indians we saw did not bother us. One event I especially remember was a severe hailstorm near Antelope Station. Some hailstones were as big as hen's eggs and we had a terrible time to hold the teams.

Upon arriving at the frontier town of Denver City, the family remained behind while father continued on to Black Hawk. Soon we followed after, taking the stagecoach. We went by way of Golden Gate, to the north of Golden and down Guy Hill. Billy Updike drove the stage and he was a wonderful driver. He could take his horsewhip and at its full length, cut the wick off a lighted candle without putting out the light. I saw him do it.

ALONZO H. ALLEN (FROM <u>PIONEER LIFE</u> <u>IN OLD BURLINGTON</u>)

I was born February 8, 1860 at Columbus, Wisconsin, and came to Colorado in 1863. In 1864, superintendent of the Overland Stage Company, Bob Spottswood, contracted with my mother to operate a "stage station" or hotel for the accommodation of passengers,

Alonzo H. Allen was born in 1860 in Wisconsin and came to Colorado in 1863. His mother operated a stage station for the Overland Stage Company, for the accommodation of passengers, drivers, stock tenders, and others connected with the stageline.
Courtesy Denver Public Library, Western History Collection

drivers, stock tenders, and others connected with the stageline. A long, roomy board and grout building was built on the east side of the road, just south of the bridge and just south of our cabin. It was built for service rather than beauty, but was comfortable enough. It was home to me during the years of my early childhood, and I have many happy memories of the days I spent there. One of my most cherished memories is of the visit to our house or "home station" of General Ulysses S. Grant, who, with his party, made a trip through the west in 1868. As I recall, also in his party, were Generals Sherman, Colfax and perhaps others. They traveled in two special coaches and we knew in advance that they were coming.

In 1865, mother had a two-story addition built onto the north end of the old house. On the ground floor were the office, dining room, living room and two large bedrooms, while upstairs were four bedrooms, large enough for two beds each. At that it was often necessary to spread blankets and buffalo robes on the floor of the dining room. At such times it was nearly impossible to let them get to bed before the departure of the midnight coaches, and it was necessary to get them up before the tables could be set for breakfast.

At the time mother was feeding the passengers, drivers, stock tenders and regular town boarders, she was using pitch pine wood for fuel in a large sheet iron range, dipping water from barrels that had been hauled from the river on sleds; doing her laundry out of doors, using wooden tubs and washboards; ironing with heavy cast iron flatirons, with no modern bathrooms and with all outbuildings quite a distance from the house.

MABEL BARBEE LEE
🌿 (FROM <u>CRIPPLE CREEK DAYS</u>) 🌿

It was chilly and daylight had just begun to break when we arrived in Florence, several hours before the stage was due to leave for Cripple Creek. We huddled on a bench in the depot surrounded by our bundles and wicker telescopes. The big trunk, which Kitty had checked, had come through safely but it would have to be held over for the next freighter into camp. After the sun came up, people gathered on the platform and strolled in and out of the room. Kitty, (my mother), was the only woman around. The roughly dressed men stared at her and two or three tried to make conversation. I managed to toy conspicuously with my silver dollar so that the passengers might turn their eyes on me instead of Kitty.

Mabel Barbee Lee was the author of a book entitled, "Cripple Creek Days," with a foreword by Lowell Thomas, who was her pupil when she was a young schoolmarm in Cripple Creek. She was the Colorado College Dean of Women from 1922-29.
Courtesy of Denver Public Library, Western History Collection

The big Concord lumbered up to the platform; at last, I had never seen such an odd, top-heavy stage outside of pictures in fairy tales. Its body was closed, with doors and windows on both sides and a driver's seat so high that it made me dizzy just to look up. Three span of horses were needed to haul the vehicle up the steep shelf road to the District, (Cripple Creek), thirty miles north. Everybody, lugging knapsacks and other possessions made a scramble to get inside or climb on top. By the time Kitty and I had gathered our belongings no space was left in the coach. The busy driver was in and out of the depot, apparently getting his orders. He was about to jump up on the seat when he suddenly noticed my mother alone, crowded out and looking as if she didn't know what to do.

"Was you aimin' to go to the Crik, lady?" he asked, smiling good-naturedly. She told him that she was but the men folks had taken up all of the room. "Well, we'll just see about that," he said, going over to the coach, "Cain't 'low no strap hangin', my load's limited to fourteen, provided a couple are lightweights."

He opened one of the doors and counted the passengers inside, "Cain't let more'n six medium sized folks on them two seats," he said, spitting and wiping his mouth on his sleeve. "Here, you two big bruisers, get up on the seat with me, make room for this little lady and her girl. Come on, git movin', ain't got all day for gabbin!"

Almost before we knew it, mother and I were sitting back comfortably on one of the two cushioned seats that faced each other. The driver cracked his whip and yelled at the horses, "Gee-Doc, giddyap there, Prince-steady-steady." The town soon vanished behind a cloud of dust.

It was early afternoon and warm for mid-October when we started, but as soon as we reached the foothills a chilly wind came up and the shadows began to deepen until only the tips of the mountains could be seen catching the last rays of sun. The three passengers facing us scowled and grumbled while Kitty dozed and glanced at me now and then to make sure that I was all right.

I began to feel drowsy at last and was about to fall asleep when one of the men across began to talk loud enough for me to hear.

"Un'stand' we're takin' that new shelf road through Phantom Canyon," he said. "Sure feels like it-dug right outa' the cliffs, they say, 'cept for a stretch along the bottom of Eight Mile Crik. "Lotsa' accidents, I hear, up above where the lead team has to be unhitched to make it around the hairpin curves, one slip an 'yer name's mud!" "Lucky it's dark," said another, "what can't be seen won't hurt nobody."

I must have fallen asleep, because for the next thing I knew the stage had stopped and Kitty was shaking me and telling me that we had come to a halfway house. After the stop to change horses, we climbed back into the coach for the final lap of our journey. "Barring accidents and other unforeseen events," the driver said, "we should arrive in camp between ten and eleven o'clock tonight." Several miles of hard pulling still lay ahead of us before we reached the settlement called Limekiln. The road was even sharper than it was below the halfway house.

What happened next was more of a bad dream than an actual occurrence. I was so tired and I couldn't open my eyes. People were cursing and arguing, and it seemed as if I was being pushed and shoved about like putty. "What's the matter, where are we going?" I asked drowsily. "Shh — be still, just hang on to me," she whispered. "It's bandits!"

I clung to her skirts for dear life as we milled around in the lantern light, watching the masked men line up the other passengers. They left Kitty until the last and when they came to her they seemed to get polite, all at once, as though it was against their principles to frisk a woman. My heart thumped with fear but curiosity burned my mind. I could see the two burly thieves with bandanas *covering all but their eyes. Their caps were pulled down and they wore heavy shirts. A lantern hung from the cartridge belt of each one together with a pistol holster. The bandits worked fast, one covering the victims with his six-shooter while the other searched them for money and jewelry.*

As the hold-up men stepped closer to us, I clutched my silver dollar tighter in my pocket. Panic gripped me as I tried to think of a safer place for it. They would see me if I slipped it into my stocking. Pretending to scratch my nose, I slid the silver dollar into my mouth. It choked me and tickled my throat until it was all I could do to keep from coughing. I felt a heavy hand on my shoulder, "Git in line there, you young whippersnapper!" a gruff voice said.

"Please, please mister," Kitty begged, "spare her, don't scare her to death!" He scowled at her for a second, and then winked as he leaned toward me and squinted as if he couldn't believe his eyes. "Well, I'll be gol-durned!" he said, as if flabbergasted, and waved to his partner. "Take a look at this sassy faced kid," he said pointing with his pistol. "Don't that beat all how she was tryin' to cheat us?"

"Guess we oughta' learn her a lesson as a warnin," the other said, pursing his lips seriously and nodding. The threat seemed to strike both men as being very funny, and they motioned the rest of the passengers to come over and look at me. They too began to snicker and even my mother seemed to be holding back a smile. I hadn't been able to close my jaws and it came to me all at once that they were laughing at the dollar lying there in plain sight in my mouth. One of the fellows reached over and patted my head. Then, without saying a word, he pulled another dollar out of the heavy satchel and slipped it in on top of the other one in my wide-open mouth.

"Next time, pug-nose," he said, chuckling and fastening the satchel again, "better keep your little mouth shut. Don't try no funny tricks, you mightn't fare as well with a fella' who ain't been brung up like a gentleman!"

Before long we could see the lights of the mines in Cripple Creek. Occasionally, the faint yellow flicker of a candle showed through a cabin window, and then some little shacks and tents with people out in front swinging lanterns. It must have been well past midnight when the sixes galloped across the flats below camp and pulled up to a stop at the Continental Hotel on Myers Avenue.

The street was crowded with men and out of the uproar of yowling dogs and pistol shots we heard yells of "Hello Sucker!" and

"Ah, there, Yokels!" and "Welcome Tenderfeet!" It was far more terrifying than being held up by robbers on the Shelf road in the dead of night.

🌿 BAYARD TAYLOR (FROM <u>A SUMMER TRIP</u>) 🌿

Denver, Colorado Territories, June 29, 1866

From Hedinger's Lake to Denver a new cut-off has recently been made, shortening the distance about twenty miles. Ours was the last coach, which passed over the old road, the stations and stock being taken up behind us and transferred across the country to their new positions. When the stations shortened to an average of ten or twelve miles and the road was well stocked, as it should be, the trip can easily be made in three days. By that time, the trains on the Pacific Railroad will be running to Fort Riley, and Twenty-four hours more will bring the travelers to St. Louis.

Our next sign of life was the evidence of death, the unfenced cemetery of Denver City, on the top of the ridge. I looked out ahead, from time to time, but could see neither horse, tree, fence, nor other sign of habitation. My fellow passengers had been loud in their praises of the place, and I therefore said nothing. Suddenly I perceived, through the dust, a stately Square Gothic tower, and rubbed my eyes with a sense of incredulity. It was really true, there was a tower, built of brick, well proportioned and picturesque.

Bayard Taylor was born in 1825 in Kennett Square, Pennsylvania. He was an American journalist and author. His poems secured him a long-standing assignment as correspondent for the New York Tribune. *He traveled extensively and was appointed as U.S. minister to Germany in 1878. He died in Berlin in 1878.*

Courtesy Denver Public Library,
Western History Collection

Dwellings and cottages rose over the dip of the ridge, on either side brick blocks began to appear, and presently we were rolling through gay, animated streets, down the vistas of which the snowy ranges in the west were shining fairly in the setting sun. The coach drew up at the Pacific Hotel, where I found a hearty welcome and good quarters, and in just four days and six hours from Fort Riley, I sat down, not to a "square meal," but to an excellent supper.

J. D. HOLLAND (FROM THE COLORADO MINER)

Holland was writing about his trip from Georgetown to Leadville.

Let the reader accompany us on a pleasant trip. Five o'clock, long has the sun shone its face across old Griffith Mountain, we take a seat in Nott's line of stages, bound for the carbonate camp and all intermediate points. We are lucky enough to get a seat with the driver, it is our favorite place, for Jehu can tell us all about the horses, and then, too, he will assist us in making way with that small vial and a pocketful of cigars. We can smoke out here and it doesn't annoy the ladies in the coach. Slowly along the road, up grade, to the Plume, which we pass just as the early risers are stirring; then, as we strike comparatively level ground, we bowl along at a lively pace. The passengers who have not been this way before gaze with wonder at the great dump piles that mark the location of mines on Sherman, Republican, and Brown Mountains. We tell them about the millions that have been taken out of these old hills and the millions that remain to reward the industrious miners in the years to come.

Along easy slopes, the road traverses the mountain side, the view down the valley is grand and beautiful, ahead of us the old Range with its curving edge seems to bid defiance to those who would seek to cross it. But the summit is reached, Loveland Pass is attained. While the horses are "blowing," we jump out and with one hand toss a rock down the Atlantic slope while casting a rock with the other hand down toward the waters of the Pacific.

Having done Leadville, we are now ready to return home. Ed Cooke and Harley Wasson have already instructed J. H. Younglove at the stage office to "fix" us, and that gentleman courteously offers us a choice of seats, but Col. Bob Spottswood "fixes" us over his line via Weston Pass to the end of the South Park Railroad, and accepting the courtesy we are assigned an outside seat by Alexander Street, the gentlemanly agent, and mount the box alongside

Col. M.O. Sherman, whom we find to be a jovial companion, as well as a number one driver.

Our trip to Fairplay is accomplished without accident or incident worthy of note. The road is in splendid condition, compared to what we found last October, the mountain division is in excellent order, but the line through the park, owing to recent heavy rains is somewhat cut up.

All aboard and off we go to Como, the end of the track, nine miles away, where we are due at four o'clock. As we leave Fairplay, a storm cloud sweeps down from the frosty summit of Mount Lincoln, and we are soon enveloped in a drenching shower of ice-cold rain; but rubber coats and buffalo robes protect the occupants of the driver's seat. We dash on, to reach Como and sunshine at one end and the same moment having made our 61 miles in ten hours.

Here we learn the train is four hours late. After waiting a long time, a cloud of smoke way off in the Park tells of the approaching train. It comes around a distant hill. It is here, and we shall get away from this delectable town before pistol popping begins in earnest.

Rocky Mountain News, *July 4, 1880*

The well-equipped fast stage of Bob Spottswood is now running from Como to Breckenridge, then over Hoosier Pass to Alma, connecting there with Wall & Witter's line for Fairplay and Leadville. Order for tickets from Como to Breckenridge, or from Como to Alma via Breckenridge, sent from the hotels by telephone to J. B. Whiting, Agent, "Wall & Witter" office, 190 Fifteenth Street, will receive prompt attention.

The largest and best hotel in Boulder is Brainard's Hotel. The only house in Boulder having commercial sample rooms and hot and cold baths.

T. C. Brainard, Proprietor

CHAPTER TEN

CITIES AND TOWNS ALONG THE TRAIL: NORTHEAST COLORADO

During the stagecoach era in Colorado, dozens of settlements were established. Mining towns throughout the mountains thrived during the last half of the nineteenth century, but many disappeared after their mining boom was over. On the other hand, dozens of tiny stops along the stage routes would eventually evolve into the towns and cities we know today. Follow along, then, as we take to the dusty roads where the stagecoaches of old were wont to travel. We will begin our search in the northeastern part of the state and work our way down through the towns in alphabetical order.

BAILEYS

Once called Baileys but now called Bailey, this small mountain town is situated in a steep canyon along the North Fork of the South Platte River. In 1885, the town included a post office, a news depot, sawmills, and some snug little cottages. Sales of timber were the town's principal business at that time.

The Denver and South Park Stageline made frequent trips between Morrison and Fairplay, stopping at Baileys en route. When the roads were improved, the Denver and South Park Stageline would pick up passengers in Denver in the morning and deliver them to Fairplay by nightfall. The same trip took forty-eight hours in the winter months.

Key
■ Stagestops
● Cities & Towns

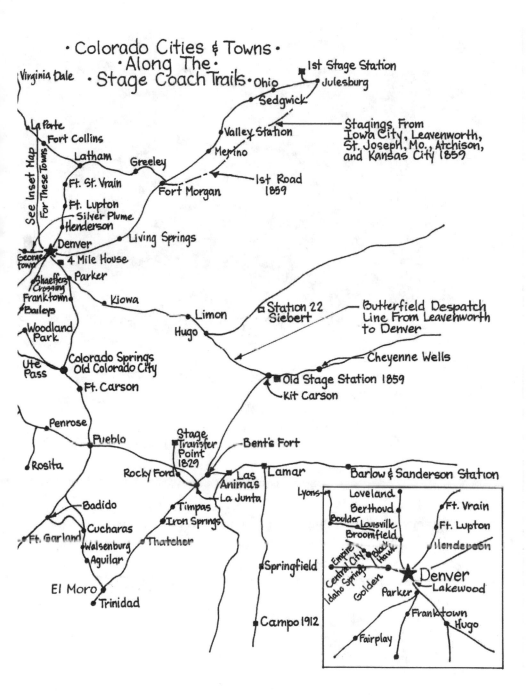

Colorado cities and towns map was drawn by Steven M. Burke

Men and women pose on and near two stagecoaches on the Eldora Line at the halfway house in Boulder Canyon (Boulder County), Colorado. Carl Talmage and John Lilly, owners of the coaches, stand near the wheels of the covered coach. (Between 1898 and 1904)
Courtesy of Denver Public Library, Western History Collection

BOULDER

In the 1880s, the population of Boulder was around 3,500. There were numerous businesses operating in the town at that time. There were two flourmills, two banks, one foundry, one smelting furnace, and dozens of small enterprises of every description.

The frontier town of Boulder had several good stagelines running to the mining camps in the local mountains. Lee and Walter Smith formed a stageline that started right after Boulder Canyon Road was extended to Nederland in 1871. Coaches ran from Boulder to Black Hawk, with a branch line up to Caribou. The station and barn were located where the Boulderado Hotel is now standing. "I can still remember playing on the old Concord stages standing out in the yard," said Martin Parsons, who grew up in Boulder.

CHAPTER 10: NORTHEAST COLORADO

DENVER

The first settlement on the site of Denver City was established in the summer of 1858. On June 7, 1859, two Concord Coaches of the Leavenworth and Pike's Peak Express arrived, to the great excitement of the residents. It was claimed to be one of the proudest days in the early history of the city. The coaches arrived over the route laid out by Jones and Russell.

The arrival propagated a great deal of rejoicing, because the Express coaches brought with them a large number of letters merely two weeks or so old, to be distributed among the intended recipients at the new mining camp. On the stages were nine passengers. The journey took fifteen days from the Missouri River to Denver City.

Denver City grew rapidly and soon became an important staging center. When new mining camps opened, mail routes came into Denver City from nearly all directions. In addition to the daily line, there were stages running south from Denver City to Old Colorado City, Pueblo, and even Santa Fe, New Mexico.

The Overland Stage to Denver City. The first coach of the Leavenworth and Pikes Peak Express Company arrived in Denver on the 7th of May, 1859. It took seven days and cost the cramped passengers $100. Each.
Harper's Weekly, January 27, 1866. Courtesy of P. David Smith

The stagecoach era in Denver City lasted about ten years. The stagecoach lines that ran in and out of Denver City in the mid-1880s were the Butterfield Overland Despatch, the Holladay Overland Mail and Express

Company, Wells Fargo and Company, John Hughes and Company, and Spottswood, Bogue and Company.

ESTES PARK

Walter A. Buckingham established the first stagecoach line from Longmont to Estes Park in 1878. From 1884 until 1893, Abner and Fred Sprague operated a stageline from Loveland to Moraine Park (near Estes), where they hauled both freight and passengers.

Haystack Boulder plummeted down and rolled onto the valley floor thousands of years ago. This boulder was seen by hundreds of weary travelers on the Overland Stage on their way from Denver to Wyoming. It is not far from one of the stage stops in Larimer County. The story is told of the hay buyer for the stage company approaching a rancher and asking if he wanted to sell the stack of hay that was down in the valley. The rancher guessed he would if the price was right but insisted the hay buyer name the price, saying that he knew the going price for hay. The buyer named a very low price, and the rancher took it. The buyer paid the money fast, before the rancher had a chance to change his mind. When the buyer went to get his hay, he stuck his fork into the hay, only to discover that the big rock had just enough hay on it to hide it. For years, local ranchers referred to it as Haystack Boulder or Haystack Rock.

Courtesy of Local History Librarian, Rheba Massey, Ft. Collins Library
Sketch by Steven M. Burke

The nearest ranch was located on the St. Vrain River some twenty-five miles distant; the nearest post office was farther downstream at Burlington (now the town of Longmont), at a stage stop on the Overland Express.

FORT COLLINS

Fort Collins was on the main route of the stagecoach line from La Porte to Virginia Dale. The town was located on the south bank of the Cache la Poudre River. The fort or stockade of that name was abandoned in 1866. The population at that time was approximately 1,000 residents.

A stagecoach is stopped on a road above a stream in Larimer County, Colorado. Men sit on and near the stagecoach and stand near the stream. Ypsilon Mountain is in the distance. 1882
Courtesy of Denver Public Library, Western History Collection

FORT MORGAN

The site of Fort Morgan is on the south bank of the South Platte River at the Junction Ranch. It was originally called "Camp Tyler," then the name was changed to "Camp Wardwell," before finally becoming the town of Fort Morgan.

The Fort Morgan cut-off was established in October of 1864 by Ben Holladay to save about forty miles and three days worth of travel to Denver. It was also used for avoiding Indian attacks along the South Platte. By December, the military officials had ordered Holladay to officially adopt this cut-off, bypassing stage stations between Fort Morgan and Latham.

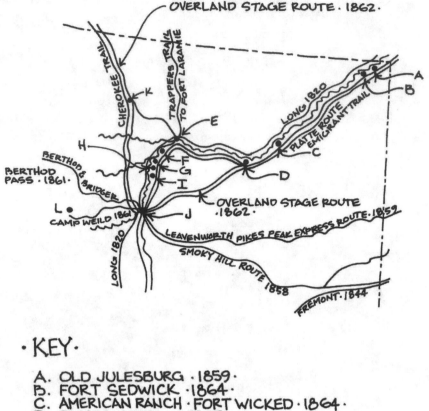

Sketch of the Overland Stage Route in 1862 drawn by Steven M. Burke

· KEY ·

A. OLD JULESBURG · 1859 ·
B. FORT SEDWICK · 1864 ·
C. AMERICAN RANCH · FORT WICKED · 1864 ·
D. CAMP WARDELL · 1865 ·
E. FORT LATHAM · 1862 ·
F. FORT ST. VRAIN · 1837 ·
G. FORT VASQUEZ · 1837 ·
H. TRAPPERS FORT
I. FORT LUPTON · 1836 ·
J. DENVER CITY ·
K. CAMP COLLINS · 1863 ·
L. CENTRAL CITY

GOLDEN CITY

In 1859, the town of Golden City was just being established. Many busy stagelines ran in and out of Golden City as it was located at the entrance into the mountains on Clear Creek — a major mining area. One stage station that appeared on the Gregory Toll Road was known as Centennial Ranch. Daniel Booten and his sister built it in 1862. The Eight-Mile House was another stage stop, restaurant, and dancehall; and it was located eight miles from Golden City. Tucker Gulch and the Guy House were two of the best-known stage stops on the road to Gregory's Gulch. Other stops were the Drew Ranch, the Michigan House, Ralston Creek Ranch, Smith Hill Stage Station, and the Coal Creek Canyon Stage Stop.

Travel from Golden City to the mountains was known as the "Mountain Route." Stages each carried between fifteen and twenty passengers a day. From Central City, shipments of gold and silver through Golden City averaged about $50,000 a week, sometimes they would go as high as $5,000 in one shipment.

The *Golden Transcript* hailed Wells Fargo's new stone building in Golden as "one of the most substantial and commodious stage stables in the country."

The old Greeley Stagecoach with Johnnie Gruber, an early day pioneer.
Courtesy Denver Public Library, Western History Collection

GREELEY

In October of 1876, Sid Probst started an enterprise with a wagon that was similar to the very earliest stagecoaches. Sid bid for the mail route from the United States Government and, upon losing, later bought it from the successful bidder. He then began a bi-weekly stage and mail run from Greeley to Julesburg. Passengers could ride from Greeley to Julesburg for $9.00. Many of Sid's passengers were beef buyers and easterners looking at what Sid advertised as "The best country in the west—and the healthiest."

JULESBURG

Julesburg is in the extreme northeastern corner of Colorado on Lodge Pole Creek. Jules Beni, a French trader, established Julesburg in 1859 as a trading post and it became an important stop along the trail even before Ben Holladay created the Overland Trail.

For a short time, Julesburg served as an important stage station for the Leavenworth and Pike's Peak Express as well as the eastern terminal of the Pony Express. Julesburg was an impressive settlement consisting of a number of buildings all constructed of hand-hewn logs. Julesburg had, in those days, a telegraph office, a store, a blacksmith shop, warehouses, stables, and homesteader's cabins — in addition to the Overland Stage Station building.

Between January and February of 1865, Indians repeatedly attacked Julesburg and the Overland Trail. They burned twelve ranches, destroyed one hundred tons of hay, and attacked a wagon train consisting of over twenty wagons. They totally destroyed all of the buildings at Julesburg, and tore down about seventy-five miles of telegraph line to the west. The burning of the station was the greatest financial loss of any station on the stageline. Ben Holladay reported to Congress losses of $115,000.

LAKEWOOD

Spottswood and McClellan's stageline route from Denver City followed portions of the old Bradford Hill road through Lakewood. It entered the present city at South Sheridan Boulevard and Morrison Road. There, on the farm of a retired sea captain named Storrs, a deep water well was available for traveling oxen teams and horses pulling the stages.

After Spottswood sold the stageline in 1880, he purchased 520 acres of land in the Bear Creek area. Seven years later he sold part of his acreage to the United States government for the site of the Fort Logan National Cemetery. He kept 160 acres.

Lakewood's last remaining stage stop is a white rectangular building straddling the crest of South Kipling Street hill where it nosedives onto Morrison Road.

LAPORTE

It was soon obvious that Denver City would become the greatest metropolis of the new Colorado gold region, and conversely, that Laporte would rapidly decline. However, in the fall of 1863, new life was infused into the town when The Overland Stageline changed its route from Lodge Pole Creek, opposite Old Julesburg, to near the site of the Cherokee City Post office, at Latham, 140 miles west of the old crossing.

CHAPTER 10: NORTHEAST COLORADO

There was a hotel in Laporte in the early days known as the Ferry House. The old stage station, used by Ben Holladay in the 1860s, was a prominent building. It was a home station, had some repair shops, and was located on the north bank of the river. The stage fare from Denver City to Laporte was twenty dollars.

Laporte soon became a bustling business and supply center for emigrants, with wagon trains and stagecoaches constantly passing through. There were four saloons, a brewery, a butcher shop, two blacksmith shops, a general store, and a hotel. Laporte was the most important settlement north of Denver City, as it contained the stage station, the County Court House, and a large variety of military, Indians, and trappers.

LATHAM

Latham, the last station on the South Platte and named in honor of Milton S. Latham (one of California's early senators), was built in 1862 at the mouth of the Cache la Poudre River. It was originally called Cherokee City Station and was probably the most important and busiest facility on the Overland Trail. It was located about one and a half miles to the east of the city limits of present day Greeley.

Unlike many of the other stations along the Overland Trail, Indians never attacked Latham; although the staff members were often frightened by reports of attacks nearby and by rumors of impending attacks.

LOUISVILLE

In *Crofutt's Grip-Sack Guide*, published in 1885, Louisville is described as "a small hamlet of about 300 persons where is located an extensive coal mine. It is in Boulder County, 36 miles northwest of Denver City."

Stagecoach transportation came before and remained many years after the Pony Express way stations had crumbled to dust. Ben Holladay's Overland Stageline took over the northern U.S. Mail route, which ran through Louisville, in 1861.

In 1863, The Rock Creek House was constructed as a "swing station" and hotel for the Overland Stageline. The "Church Station" was operated by George and Sarah Church, and was the slow freight swing station. Rock Creek was the fast freight swing station and stage stop and was owned and operated by Thomas Lindsay.

LYONS

Stagecoach travel in the late 1800s was a busy industry in and around Lyons. Gilbert and Hubbell operated a Concord coach pulled by four horses out of Longmont. It was a forty-mile journey up the canyon with a stop at Lyons at mile twenty-three.

Occasionally passengers would have to help push the stagecoach out of ruts in the road. When they reached the halfway point, the passengers were much relieved to have a respite from the tiring journey. When a new road was built in 1883 from Lyons to Estes Park over Rowell Hill, it shortened the trip somewhat.

Mr. William N. Hubbell and his family bought out Mr. Gilbert's interest and established the Longmont-Estes Park Stageline.

James Archie, a stagecoach driver who drove from Estes Park to Lyons, said that Arbuckle Hill was so steep he would have to tie his passengers down with a rope to keep them from tumbling out. The Arbuckle was a popular resort at the time located on the Longmont Dam Road.

Rowell Hill, also known as "Roll Over Hill," was so steep that a 2200-foot gain in altitude was made in slightly more than two miles. It severely stressed the horses, the passengers, and the drivers. The stage turned over repeatedly on this stretch of road, and it was known to have claimed at least one life.

NEDERLAND

Nederland is a little town located on Middle Boulder Creek in Boulder County. In 1880, the Caribou Silver Mill and the Gold Quartz Mill was situated here. Stagecoaches from Central City, Caribou, and Boulder passed through this quaint little town where in addition to the mills; several hotels, stores, and a sawmill thrived.

PARKER

Parker can trace its colorful history to the establishment of the Pine Grove Post Office by Alfred Butters in the 1860s. Early traders, trappers, gold seekers, and frontiersmen used the old Indian trail that ran next to Cherry Creek. The trail was known by many names including Cherokee Trail, the South Branch of the Smoky Hill Trail, and a branch of the Trapper's Trail. When stagecoaches began operating in Colorado the trail became known as the West Cherry Creek Stage Road and the Denver and Santa Fe Stage Road.

James Sample Parker, a bullwhacker and station manager, opened the "Twenty Mile House." It was the first official post office in the settlement. Before the railroad arrived, the Butterfield Overland Despatch line ran through Parker with stops at Sulphur Creek and the "Twenty Mile House."

SHAEFFER'S CROSSING

Thirty-five miles southwest of Denver is a "wide spot in the road" called Shaffer's Crossing. Shaffer's Crossing was first mentioned as a waystop for the stagelines in 1860. In 1870, the St. Louis House began operation.

Several passengers board a horse-drawn stagecoach in front of the Nanichant Inn (Perry Park Hotel) in Perry Park (Douglas County), Colorado. 1901.
Courtesy Denver Public Library, Western History Collection

The barn that was built for the old stage stop is still standing. The structure was erected with wooden pegs to hold it together.

VIRGINIA DALE

Barely a hop, skip, and jump from the Wyoming border lies the small community of Virginia Dale, which was once a very busy stage stop on the Overland Stage line. Much colorful history happened in this location. An old stage station still survives and the Virginia Dale Community Club is restoring the building.

The infamous Jack Slade built the stage station in 1862 in an impressive setting among granite outcroppings. Slade named the station after his wife, Virginia, and he served as the first station agent. The post office at Virginia Dale opened briefly in 1868, then closed, and opened again from 1871 to 1967.

CHAPTER ELEVEN

CITIES AND TOWNS ALONG THE TRAIL: SOUTHEAST COLORADO

outheast of the historic Overland Trail (which generally followed today's Interstate 25), south of the historic Smoky Hill Trail (today's Interstate 70), and in the middle of the legendary Santa Fe Trail (Highway 50) is the oldest and most historic section of Colorado. It's also known as the Comanche National Grasslands.

Many of the settlements in this part of Colorado were railroad towns; that is, they were built as the railroad track progressed into Colorado. As a result, quite a few present-day towns in southeastern Colorado didn't exist in the stagecoach era. Some cities, such as Pueblo and Walsenburg, have very little information in regard to stagecoaching. Stagelines undoubtedly traveled through these towns and had terminals and connecting lines, but other historical events have taken precedent over stagecoaching.

AGUILAR

Aguilar is located alongside Interstate 25, between Walsenburg and Trinidad. It marks the entrance of the Apishapa Valley in southeastern Colorado, and leads to the San Isabel National Forest, the beautiful snow capped peaks of the Sangre de Cristo Range and the majestic Spanish Peaks.

With the designation of Aguilar's Main St. and County Road 46 to Cordova Pass as part of the scenic highway of legends, the preservation of this area will prove more vital to the local economy. Many historic buildings have been lost, such as the "Foster House Stagecoach Station" east of Aguilar and the adobe home of Jose Ramon Aguilar, who the town was named after.

BENT'S OLD FORT

Until the time of the gold rush in Colorado, the Indians along the Arkansas River were only occasionally hostile to the white minority that was infiltrating their land. After 1858, however, the Southern Cheyenne and the Arapaho watched apprehensively as the long winding wagon trains traveled what was known as the River Road. The Indians grew restless, so the whites begged Washington, D.C., for protection. The Army moved in and secured the area by building a fort.

In the spring of 1861, Bent's Old Fort became a busy stage station on the official mail route to Santa Fe. The United States Postmaster General decided to use the "Military Road" instead of the Cimarron Cut-off, because the Indians had destroyed much of the mail going on that route. The new route went southwest up Timpas Creek, down to Trinidad, and then crossed Raton Pass. The Missouri Stage Company renovated old stations and built new ones, completing the route as far as Bent's Old Fort.

Colonel Jared L. Sanderson and his wife moved in to manage Bent's Old Fort Stage Station, and by July 1861, meals were being served. In 1903, Colonel Sanderson remembered many details of the stage station at the old fort; the most astonishing of which was that he personally asked William Bent for permission to use the old fort as a stage stop. He remembered the walls were newly whitewashed, and the kitchen and the dining room were on the south side of the fort.

Although Bent's Old Fort had been an official stage station on the mail route as early as 1861, its first official postmaster was not appointed until

Photo of Bent's Old Fort.

Author's Photo

Edward Dorris, a stagecoach driver, died of a sunstroke or a heart attack enroute to Bent's Old Fort, a Barlow and Sanderson stagecoach station in the 1860s. Like others who had gone before him, the hardship of life on the Santa Fe Trail ended here at Bent's Old Fort. Of the thirteen graves located in the cemetery here, twelve are covered with adobe bricks, while Dorris' grave is covered with limestone and marked.

Author's Photo Collection

June 4, 1863. Most postmasters obtained their jobs through political pull, and Lewis Barnum had pull. His brother was, at one time, a partner in the stage company, and his wife was the niece of Colonel Albert G. Boon, the Indian agent who had succeeded William Bent.

There were many opinions of the stage facilities at Bent's Fort, which appeared in newspapers at that time. One reporter noted that the company had converted the fort into, "a very complete and comfortable station," and gave special praise to Arthur Hill, who had charge of the coach from Denver City. Another reporter disliked the stage companies, the coaches, the weather, and the fort; but he was elated when Arthur Hill announced the arrival of the incoming stage by blowing a "fish horn solo." Some Episcopal Bishops were taking a trip from Denver City through Bent's Fort to Santa Fe and recalled the following experience:

> *We left this comfortable home about sundown and arrived at Bent's Old Fort at 6 a.m.. Not a military, but an old trading post,*

as these strong adobe buildings were erected in early times for the protection against the Indians. We have several posts and they are all quite formidable in size and appearance.

Here we lie over 24 hours for the coach from the east for Santa Fe. It is a very uncomfortable place; the dirt floors, the hard living and the bedbugs together present an array of inconveniences; appalling to my New York brother, and though nothing new to me, not greatly to be desired. The Santa Fe Coach from the east has come in. I am sure that it would both surprise and amuse our eastern friends to see a place such as this, some had beds and bugs, some the floor, and quite a number the ground or straw in the corral.

We are over the river and off for Santa Fe but what a trial to get off, never have I seen imposition upon passengers as that practiced by the Kansas City and Santa Fe Stage Company. There is no limit, either, as to passengers or express matter and the result is that as in our own case, they pack us in for a ride of four hundred miles without the slightest chance to stretch our legs.

Travel around Bent's Old Fort became more difficult when the seriousness of the White-Indian fighting heightened in late 1864. The local minister, Reverend Adams, feared for his life and left the fort to settle near Cañon City, so probably no minister was at the fort when, on June 21, 1865, Edward Dorris, a stagecoach driver, died of either a sunstroke or heart attack enroute to the fort. The fort at that time was a Barlow and Sanderson stagecoach station. Dorris' grave still stands outside the reconstructed fort in memory of the man who endured the hardships of life on the Santa Fe Trail.

CAÑON CITY

Promoters of the new town of Cañon City, the tiny settlement on the Arkansas River, expected the little town to provide services to nearby mining camps similar to those provided by Denver City and Old Colorado City. They were therefore happy to hear that the Santa Fe mail route and the Missouri Stage Company would run an express line to their town. Miller and Evans, proprietors of the express coach, announced on December 1, 1860, that the well-known express company of Hinkley and Company were now prepared to transport gold dust and light freight to and from Cañon City to any part of the United States and Europe at reduced rates. Passengers and freight would leave Denver City for Cañon City every Friday.

Men, women and children ride a stagecoach with a four-horse team in Cañon City, Colorado. Stagecoach features ornate flourishes, lamps, and a roof rail; boy with a baby donkey stands by the wheel. Brick Methodist Church has stone, angular voussoirs, and ornamental dormers. (Between 1873 and 1880)
Courtesy Denver Public Library, Western History/Genealogy Dept.

Cañon City completed the "Shelf Road" in 1892, linking Leadville and the Arkansas Valley with the district. A trip along the Shelf Road took six hours upgrade and four hours downgrade. Tolls ranged from thirty cents for a horse and rider to $1.75 for a six-horse stagecoach.

CASCADE

Manitou Springs, once called Boiling Springs, served as the entrance to Ute Pass. Trappers and freighters used the old worn Indian trail to enter the mountains and travel to the mining towns near the Continental Divide. Once called the Ute Trail, it soon became known as Ute Pass. It followed the swift moving "Fountaine de Bouile," now known as Fountain Creek. Stagecoaches later traversed this trail.

Winding through the rugged walls of Ute Pass is the town of Cascade, which began as a log house and dirty saloon. Ute Pass traffic helped it prosper. By 1888, there was a plush hotel named Ramona after Helen Hunt Jackson's book. Tourists from near and far enjoyed the ninety-three rooms, elegant ladies parlor, the colorful ballroom, and the cool mountain air from the 200-foot veranda. Eventually, Cascade became the entrance to the Pike's Peak Toll Road.

CHEYENNE WELLS

The Smoky Hill Trail (also called the Butterfield Trail and the Starvation Trail) followed the Smoky Hill River. It crossed Cheyenne County from east to west. Lt. John C. Fremont is known to have used this trail as early as 1844. When gold was discovered on Cherry Creek in 1859, the trail was promoted as the most direct route to Denver City.

The trail split near "Old Wells" (about five miles north of present-day Cheyenne Wells) into north and south forks. The north fork of the trail went northwest from "Old Wells" Station through Deering Wells Station, Big Springs Station, and David Wells Station, and eventually to Denver. The north and south trails joined again near Hugo.

The Butterfield Overland Despatch (spelled occasionally with either an "e" or an "i") began operation in Cheyenne County in 1865. In 1866, Wells Fargo and Company purchased The Butterfield Overland Dispatch, but Wells Fargo and Company sold it in 1869. The progression of the railroad

A group of people sit on and stand near a stagecoach parked outside the Antlers Hotel in Colorado Springs, El Paso County, Colorado. The stagecoach is hitched to a seven-horse team that is draped with a banner that reads, "The Evening News." A man stands on a ladder near the hotel entrance. The entrance is decorated with greenery and bunting. 1890-1898

Courtesy Denver Public Library, Western History Collection

into Colorado led to the eventual end of the stagecoach business. In March 1870, the community at "Old Cheyenne Wells" (the stage station) moved five miles to meet the railroad at the present day site.

COLORADO SPRINGS

When gold was discovered in the Colorado Mountains in 1859, many of the new arrivals earned their living by mining or through businesses that supported mining. Colorado Springs had a good wagon road to South Park, so business was attracted to this area. The City of Denver also continued to grow, so when a better road was built from Denver City to the mining areas of South Park, many of the mine-related businesses moved there.

In 1917, Colorado Springs and Old Colorado City became one town. Tourism was popular, especially since the area had a good reputation for being a healthy environment to live. In 1869, the settlement of Edgerton

View of Bennett Avenue, the Hundley Stage, and the Palace Hotel, in Cripple Creek, Colorado. Men stand by signs: "Postal Telegraph Office," "C.T.& T. Co. Coal Office (Colorado Trading and Transfer)," "Midland Terminal Ry. Freight and Ticket Office," "Fremont Grocery and Supply Co. (E.F. McCloskey Mngr.)," and "Monaco Restaurant." 1894 or 1895
Courtesy Denver Public Library, Western History Collection

boasted a stage station. The stage traveled from Denver City through Colorado Springs to Pueblo.

CRIPPLE CREEK

For several years in the 1890s, Cripple Creek was one of the largest staging centers in the country. Coaches ran into Cripple Creek from Florissant and Cañon City. Florence's stage station closed when a railroad was built from the Midland Railway. The railway was a real engineering feat as it wound its course around so many mountain peaks and up through the canyons and gulches into the camp.

The old Cripple Creek Stage Road was a route completed at the turn of the century, which ultimately transported people and gold by stagecoach to and from the Cripple Creek and Victor mining areas to Colorado Springs. The road had a very rich history and was an engineering marvel. Much of the roadway had been carved, literally, out of the mountainside.

David Wood, an experienced freighter, operated the first stageline into the camp. It was a twice daily line of four- and six-horse Concords. Later the line changed to a single daily six-horse line. A.W. Alexander succeeded Wood.

The year 1894 was a good one for the Kuykendall Transportation Company. The company carried into and out of Cripple Creek, in one year,

"On the road to Cripple Creek." Horse teams, stagecoaches, and wagons are on the Florissant to Cripple Creek Road in Teller County, Colorado. 1880-1900

Courtesy Colorado Historical Society

Stagecoach "No. 7 U.S. Mail" drawn by team of six horses, Teller County, Colorado; shows driver seated on Concord coach, another with long coat stands next to left rear horse; winter scene with snow patches on foreground dirt and cover on background slope; evergreens middleground, behind stagecoach.

Courtesy Denver Public Library, Western History Collection

37,742 passengers. The largest number of passengers ever carried in and out of Cripple Creek in one day was 740. In that year it was not uncommon to see fifteen to twenty-five passengers coming into camp on a single stage three times a day from the Midland Railroad.

It is not known when the last stagecoaches actually traveled the old stage road. Rumor had it that some early residents remember having seen a stagecoach coming down the old road as late as 1911. If they did, it was a very unusual occurrence, since the Short Line Railroad accommodated most transportation between Cripple Creek and Colorado Springs after 1905.

FLORISSANT

Hundreds of tourists enjoyed visiting the bustling gold camps, and Florissant was a favorite. Several excursion trains ran daily along the "Gold Belt Line." The Hundley Stage route between Florissant and Cripple Creek linked that mining district with the Colorado Midland Railroad and Colorado Springs. Today, Teller County Road 1, between Cripple Creek and Florissant, follows this historic stagecoach and wagon route.

The Stage from Divide.

"The Stage From Divide" shows the stagecoach as it descends from an upper trail, the horses giving their all.

Courtesy of P. David Smith

Florissant saw the daily arrival and departure of numerous stagecoaches and freight wagons destined for the gold camps. Indians and white folk alike mingled, and easterners and miners both trod her streets.

FORT CARSON

The land on which Fort Carson was built was never the permanent home of any Indian tribe, although many tribes, such as the Utes, Comanches, Kiowa, Cheyenne, Arapaho, and the Sioux, did pass through the country. The decline in the Indian population came in 1861, when the government made a treaty with the Cheyenne and the Arapaho. The tribes, according to the treaty, would give up some 80,000 square miles, which included what is now Fort Carson.

The tribes were to get $450,000, to be paid in fifteen annual payments. Reserved for their use was a tract of land along both sides of the Arkansas River and a portion of southeast Colorado. By 1869, hundreds of U.S. Cavalry soldiers were in the region and most of the Indians had left.

In 1873, the first stage road to cross Fort Carson was built. It carried passengers and freight from Denver City to Cañon City. Gold discoveries in Colorado led to the need for a better and faster route to Denver City. The demand for transportation was so great that stages began running day and night, stopping only long enough to change horses and for passenger meals. Even though a new stage route was built, outlaws continued to plague the lightly protected stages, and "traffic jams" were often created along the route by grazing buffalo.

A major stop on the old route was the stage station of Glendale, located half a mile outside the southwest boundary of the Carson reservation at the junction of the Red and Beaver Creeks. When a dam broke one rainy night in 1920, a wall of water swept through and destroyed the stage stop.

FORT GARLAND

Built in 1858, Fort Garland replaced old Fort Massachusetts, located just six miles to the north. Fort Massachusetts proved to be poorly located strategically and vulnerable to extreme weather. Fort Garland was built of adobe and was named for Brevet Brigadier General John Garland. Built on land that was part of the Sangre de Cristo Land Grant, it was leased by the United States Government.

On Barlow and Sanderson's coaches, passengers were bound by rules such as those posted at the stagecoach exhibit just off the parade grounds in the Fort Garland Museum:

Adherence to the Following Rules Will Insure a Pleasant Trip for All

Abstinence from liquor is requested, but if you drink, share the bottle. To do otherwise makes you appear selfish and unneighborly.

If ladies are present, gentlemen are urged to forego smoking cigars and pipes, as the odor is repugnant to the gentle sex. Chewing tobacco is permitted, but spit with the wind, not against it.

Gentlemen must refrain from the use of rough language in the presence of ladies and children.

Buffalo robes are provided for your comfort during cold weather. Hogging robes will not be tolerated and the offender will be made to ride with the driver.

Don't snore loudly while sleeping or use your fellow passenger's shoulder for a pillow; he or she may not understand and friction may result.

Firearms may be kept on your person for emergencies. Do not fire for pleasure or shoot at wild animals as the sound frightens the horses.

In the event of runaway horses, remain calm, leaping from the coach in panic will leave you injured, at the mercy of the elements, hostile Indians, and hungry coyotes.

Forbidden topics of discussion are stagecoach robberies and Indian uprisings.

Gents guilty of unchivalrous behavior toward lady passengers will be put off the stage. It's a long walk back. A word to the wise is sufficient.

So there you are—have a good trip!

KIT CARSON

Kit Carson, namesake of the famous western scout, guide, trapper, and Indian fighter, was founded on the eastern plains in 1838. In 1870, Kit Carson was a boisterous town of saloons, dance halls, and gambling. Almost every grown man had two six-shooters hanging from his belt. This town was an important shipping point for cattle in the early 1870s. In 1872, Kit Carson developed into a trade and supply outpost, which provided for stage companies and trading outfits.

The town of Kit Carson had two locations. The original site was located near the site where Kit Carson traded with the Indians. The arrival of the railroad determined the present site. Destroyed by fire three times, twice by the torches of Indians, and once by corrousing cowboys, the town's citizens expressed their determination to survive by rebuilding the town.

CHAPTER 11: SOUTHEAST COLORADO

There is an Old Trails Monument located just north of Kit Carson on State Highway 59 that reads:

Smoky Hill Trail — famous emigrant and stage road between Kansas City and Denver. Stations and stock were moved to this shortened northern route in 1866. Traveled by pioneers, soldiers, and the Wells Fargo and Company Express Line. Big Springs Station 2.4 miles west. Stagecoach service was withdrawn upon completion of the railroad, but wagon traffic continued thereafter.

OLD COLORADO CITY

The Colorado Trail (from what is now Colorado Springs to South Park) was a well-worn path traveled by mountain men, trappers, and the Plains Indians, who annually traveled west to fight with the Ute Indians over hunting grounds in South Park. It was the only practical route along the Front Range of the Rocky Mountains to the ever growing and prospering gold fields in South Park.

By the winter of 1860, there were eight women and three hundred male residents in Old Colorado City. Lucy Maggard of Auraria opened a facility that became known as Mother Haggard's Boarding House. It was located near the present intersection of Pikes Peak Avenue near Twenty-eighth Street. It was used by stage passengers, as it was near the stage road between Colorado Springs and Denver City that extended along Camp Creek.

The first hotel in Old Colorado City was a large two-story log house built in the spring of 1860 by Green Price of Missouri. Many Denver stagecoaches stopped at this famous hotel. H.T. Weibling of Denver secured the first mail contracts and drove the first stage into Old Colorado City. The halfway house between Colorado Springs and Denver was known as Coberly's and was located on the east branch of Plum Creek just over the divide, northeast of Old Colorado City. The stage stopped here overnight. Another tavern on Monument Creek was known as "Dirty Woman's Ranch," where travelers were glad to put up when night and storms overtook them.

To protect its historic value, Old Colorado City was designated a National Historic District in 1983. The Old Colorado City Historical Society was established to preserve the memory of Old Colorado City (1859-1917), to encourage research, preserve photographs and other memorabilia, and to maintain the unique culture and spirit of the west side Colorado Springs.

TRINIDAD

The Trinidad area is rich with history reaching back into the early 1800s, when trappers and mountain men discovered this beautiful place.

In 1865, former mountain man Richens Lacy "Uncle Dick" Wooton and his partner, George C. Mc Bride, made an agreement with Lucien Maxwell (a major New Mexico rancher) to build a toll road over Raton Pass. For months they blasted and removed rock and built bridges, finally making a passable road for twenty-seven miles. They built a tollbooth and charged $1.50 per wagon, twenty-five cents per horseman, and five cents for other animals. Native Americans and soldiers passed by free.

Trinidad was officially incorporated in 1876, just a few months before Colorado became a state. That year about 15,000 tons of freight passed over Uncle Dick's toll road.

In April 1867, a *Rocky Mountain News* reporter showered praise on the newly formed Denver and Santa Fe Stageline that connected Trinidad with Denver City. He was impressed by the fact that the line had excellent horses and that the time of the trip had been cut to a mere thirty-six hours. The reporter also described his stay at the stage's Trinidad hotel, the Davis and Barracough, by calling it the finest he had seen since leaving Denver City.

In the spring of 1867, the competition between stagelines providing service to Trinidad began heating up. Before the Denver and Santa Fe Stageline, the only stage route between Denver City and Trinidad was the Barlow and Sanderson Company that passed through Bent's Old Fort some ninety miles northeast.

At the beginning of 1867, a young Civil War veteran from Boston traveled to Trinidad to set up shop for the new Denver and Santa Fe Stageline. His name was Joseph Davis. He stayed for a time at William R. Walker's hotel, which was on the corner of today's Main and Maple Streets. The Walker Hotel was the stop for the Barlow and Sanderson Stagecoaches.

WOODLAND PARK

In the 1880s Woodland Park became a town because of the fast growing demand for lumber. In 1887, John A. Himebaugh ran the post office, became the town's first postmaster, cared for horses for the stagecoach line, and took in overnight guests traveling by stage. A buckboard came through with mail from Old Colorado City to Fairplay once a week. It took three days each way. It was rumored that Mr. Himebaugh had to get out with lanterns on dark nights to help wagons through the marshy bogs. Because of the mud, portions of the stageline were covered with logs and placed side by side to help the stages and wagons get through.

The Lynch Ranch on South Forty Road now owns this property. Although the logs have long since disappeared, the barn on the ranch is still the original one that housed the horses for the stagecoach line.

CITIES AND TOWNS ALONG THE TRAIL: NORTHWEST COLORADO

he Ute Indian tribe were the first known inhabitants of Northwestern Colorado, as well as the first known tribe to call the Rocky Mountains home. This area has always been sparsely inhabited but here important discoveries were made. Some of the places in this part of Colorado deserve some recognition, even though they cannot be classified as towns or cities.

BERTHOUD PASS

It is amazing that this famous crossing did not play a bigger part in the history of the region. The Indians neglected traveling the pass for reasons known only to them. Explanations as to why Berthoud Pass escaped the notice of trappers and mountain men remain unknown.

Edward Louis Berthoud came to Colorado in 1860 with his wife to seek opportunities for making money. He had not seen the Colorado Mountains, and he was not much of an outdoorsman. On one occasion, he made the acquaintance of the famous guide, Jim Bridger. The two of them searched for and found a route through the mountains to Middle Park, and they later named it "Berthoud Pass."

The first year the pass was opened, Captain Lewis De Witt Clinton Gaskill lived on the summit of the pass in a house made of hand-hewn logs. The Captain and his family occupied the house for over a year after the road was opened in 1874. They collected toll money and sheltered travelers who were victims of severe snowstorms. In 1874, the dirt trail became a stage road that led to Hot Sulphur Springs and many towns beyond.

The building was located across the road from the present Berthoud Pass marker, but no trace of it remains.

ASPEN

According to *Crofutt's Grip-Sack Guide of 1885*:

> *Aspen is the county seat of Pitkin County. The valley in which Aspen and the Roaring Fork are located affords a fine stock range, but the principal occupation of the people living here is mining. We have learned that a stageline is being established at once.*
>
> *Elk, deer, bear, and many other kinds of furred and feathered game are abundant in the nearby mountains, while trout snap at fishermen's bait in every little stream.*
>
> *Aspen is situated due west from Leadville, a thirty-mile journey as the crow flies, forty miles by trail, and fifty-eight and a half miles by Stage. Stage fare from Leadville to Aspen is $22.00.*

A horse-drawn stagecoach is parked in front of the Hotel Jerome in Aspen, Pitkin County, Colorado. "Trowbridge and Sweet Livery" is painted on the side of the stagecoach.

Courtesy Colorado Historical Society

BLACK HAWK

In the 1880s the mines were booming at Black Hawk, and the hills and valleys were scattered with stamp mills, engine houses, shops, and offices. Six horses were needed to pull the coach from Black Hawk to Mountain City because the grade was so steep. The trip from Denver City to Black Hawk took an astonishing amount of time — seventy-eight hours. The stages passed through towns set so close together that it was difficult to tell one from the other.

During the fall and winter of 1863, deep snow made it necessary to replace the coach's wheels with runners. The coaches with runners took much longer to reach their destination. During that winter, a coach upset at Clear Creek after its rear runners dropped into a deep rut covered with snow. The stagecoach was thrown fifteen feet into a gulch and the driver and a passenger were severely injured.

On May 28, 1864, a snowstorm of such violence occurred, that some of the stage horses died from exhaustion. Westbound and eastbound coaches were not allowed to travel until fresh livestock was sent down from Denver the following week.

Later, after the road improved, a daily stage ran between Denver and Black Hawk, leaving Black Hawk at 7:30 a.m. and arriving in Denver City at 10:00 p.m. — greatly improved service and faster transportation, to be sure.

BRECKENRIDGE

In the early 1880s, six major stagecoach lines linked Breckenridge to the outside world. The better lines used four- and six-horse Concord coaches and charged their passengers between twelve and fifteen cents per mile. Some of the routes linked Breckenridge with Hot Sulphur Springs in Middle Park once a week, Breckenridge to Kokomo — by way of Frisco — three times a week, and Como to Hamilton to Breckenridge for a distance of eighteen miles over Boreas Pass that was undergone six days a week.

Some determined individuals started their own local stagelines, such as the one implemented by "Bronco" Dave Braddock. His line ran from Breckenridge to Swan City, Delaware Flats, and Galena Gulch along the Swan River. Later, his routes expanded, and he included Lincoln City in French Gulch.

The *Summit County Journal* reported that, "The irrepressible Braddock, in order to keep open the road from Braddockville to Swan City, during the late winter, had to shovel nearly the whole distance."

The trip was a delight in the summertime, however, as a passenger remarked to *The Rocky Mountain News*, in June of 1880, "At Como, through the courtesy of Colonel Bob Spottswood, I boarded one of the splendid Concord coaches of the pioneer stageline and finished the journey to Breckenridge, a distance of 17 miles, in three and one half hours. The beautiful scenery on both sides made the trip short and charming."

CARBONDALE

About one and a half miles east of present day Carbondale, Bill Dinkel and Bob Zimmerman owned a store and stage station, which they named "Dinkels." The stage route ran through Carbondale, so, when the town founders surveyed the town site, they used the stage road for their Main Street. An eating establishment was built and operated for the convenience of the stageline on the east end of Main Street.

Barlow and Sanderson ran the first stagecoaches bi-weekly but quickly altered their schedule to allow for more runs. At one time, it was reported that Kit Carson operated a daily stageline on this road.

CENTRAL CITY

Ben Holladay held an unyielding ambition to extend his stageline far beyond the plains. In 1862, the opportunity presented itself for him to secure the mail route between Denver and mining towns in the Colorado Rockies. His first new branch line ran from Denver City to Central City, which was an important mining center at that time.

The thirty-five mile route from Denver to Central City was bordered by high bunch grass, where cattle and horses thrived, but the area was also known as the Colorado's gold mining belt. Along the Golden City route, the stage passed by impressive, high-walled canyons, then crossed steep hills to arrive at Black Hawk.

The Butterfield Overland Dispatch line became intense competition for the Holladay line on the Central City route. A price war ensued in which Holladay cut back fare prices from ten dollars a trip to one dollar for a ride to Denver from Central City.

Alas, in 1867, the mining industry began to fade, and many residents were forced to move on. In the valley that included Central City, Mountain City, and Black Hawk, abandoned mills could be seen everywhere. Missouri City, located west of Central City, was nearly a ghost town — with empty houses, rusting mills, and silent flumes everywhere.

COMO

South Park had adequate stage stations for providing meals and overnight lodging during the 1860s. One of the earliest stations was called "Eight-mile House" and was erected near Como on Tarryall Creek. It survived for over twenty years. Later when the train arrived at Como, it was met by enterprising stagelines, who delivered the train passengers to their destinations in the various mountain towns and mining camps.

DILLON

The daughter of a prominent Dillon pioneer, Mrs. Anna Emore once proclaimed "Old Dillon" to be quite a lively place. On Main Street, there were four saloons, one pool hall, two general stores, a butcher shop, a drug store, a barbershop, and two blacksmith shops.

Chauncey Carlisle Warren and his wife, Mary Elizabeth, moved to the new town of Dillon in the 1880s. They opened a stage stop, which became a popular place for travelers and locals as well. Their business was located on a busy stage route between Georgetown and Leadville. Because of their hospitality and popularity, they were able to buy and operated the Warren Hotel in Dillon.

In the winter of 1898-1899, a gigantic snowstorm buried old Dillon and Breckenridge with snow so deep as to completely cover the roofs of two-story buildings. All travel ceased, and merchants' supplies ran low because they had failed to stock enough goods in the fall. Despite the deep snow, Kremmling grocer Tracy Tyler sent food and other much-needed supplies on the Kremmling-Dillon stageline. Only by the efforts of determined and heroic stage drivers were supplies able to be delivered and the town saved.

EMPIRE

In *Frank Fossett's Tourist Guide of 1880*, the following description of Empire is given:

> *Empire is a mining town in Clear Creek County, four miles from Georgetown. The Middle Park Stageline passes through this place. A few miles west of Berthoud Pass, leading over the 'Snowy Range' lies the small town of Empire. The town is one mile above the railway station. Valuable gold placers and lode veins are worked in the vicinity, and from one to three quartz mills are always at work. The distance from Denver City is 48 miles; Idaho Springs, 11 miles. The population is 250 with an elevation of 8583 ft. above sea level.*

FRASER

Crofutt's Grip-Sack Guide to Colorado in 1885 describes Fraser thusly:

> *Frazer is a town in Grand County and is situated on the Frazer River. It consists of a hotel, post office and stockmen's ranch, all*

in one building. It is also a stage station on the road between Georgetown and Hot Sulphur Springs. Frazer is commonly called "Cozzen's Hotel," where are provided the best accomodations for tourists in the park. The hunting and fishing in the vicinity are par excellence.

It can be reached by stage from Georgetown; fare $3.00; from Denver, by rail and stage, fare $6.45.

FAIRPLAY

In 1879 the town of Fairplay, located in South Park, was a stop for freight companies headed to and from Denver City. It was a gathering place for miners and ranchers from miles around. Fairplay had a number of businesses at that point in time, such as the County Courthouse, a brewery, schoolhouse, the Fairplay Hotel, the Bergh House, a dozen or more stores, a smelter, a bank, and, of course, quite a few saloons. The population of Fairplay in the summer months was about 800 residents in 1883.

In the *Park County Echoes,* Clare Fanning wrote,

> *Stage coach travel through South Park was enhanced with better and more elegant coaches as the intense migrations of the 1860s and 1870s developed intricate networks of routes. Stageline*

Old Stage barn on Original Site.
Courtesy of South Park Historical Foundation

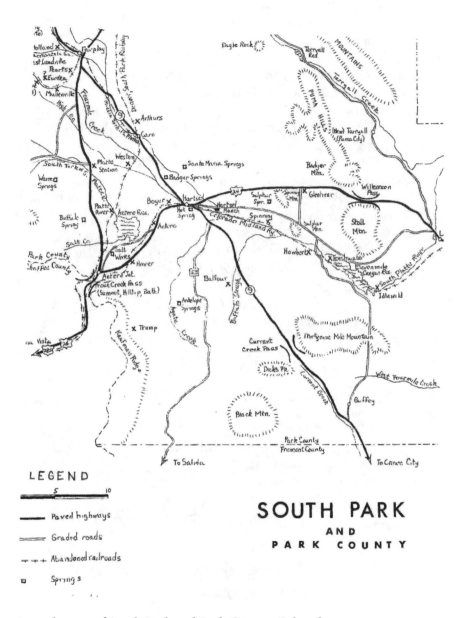

An early map of South Park and Park County, Colorado.
Courtesy of South Park Historical Foundation

drivers were held to high standards of safety and honesty. With over a dozen arrivals and departures a day from Fairplay, stageline owners would compete to have the most comfortable and pleasant surroundings within their coaches.

Spottswood and McClellan owned one of the most prosperous stagelines. They frequently used six-horse coaches, and when their most elegant coach arrived in Fairplay, the newspaper printed that it had a name: "Perley." Bob Spottswood named this particular coach after a long-time friend and stagecoach driver, as a tribute to their friendship.

In July of 1870, the trip to South Park was called "an easy excursion" on a daily stage being operated in Fairplay by John Hughes and Company. In 1872, a correspondent for *The Rocky Mountain News* reported on the stage experience to and from Fairplay:

> *The Colorado Stage Company runs tri-weekly from here to Denver City, Colorado Springs, and Breckenridge; and weekly to Cañon City. R. B. Newitt carries passengers and the mail twice a week from here to Oro City, via Chubb's rancho, Granite, Cache Creek and Twin Lakes. The entire route lies amid beautiful scenery and the accomodations are in every way reasonable. There is,*

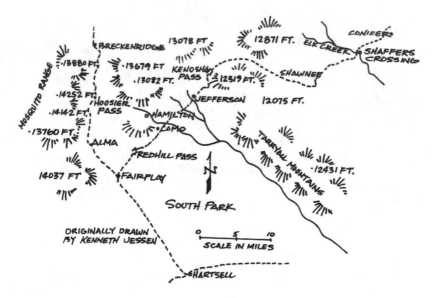

A sketch of the mountain ranges and towns in Park County by Steven M. Burke.

Originally drawn by Kenneth Jessen

Men in hats and overcoats pose beside a horse-drawn stagecoach in front of Douglas Mountain in Jefferson County near Georgetown, Colorado. Shows snow on the ground and men in the driver's seat wrapped in blankets. 1867
Courtesy Denver Public Library, Western History Collection

> *besides, a weekly mail, which runs from here to Saguache. Thus it will be seen that Fairplay is not seriously lacking in communication with the surrounding country, both in and out of the mountains*

FRISCO

Frisco! The name shouts excitement; it echoes California's gold rush and the fever pitch of growth in San Francisco in 1849. There were several differing accounts as to how Frisco was named. One version states that H.A. Recen built the first hand-hewn log cabin in Frisco in 1873, and that a government Indian scout chopped off the log over the cabin door and wrote "Frisco City" on the rough surface.

Stagelines posted their schedules in Frisco as follows:

> *Breckenridge to Kokomo via Frisco (twenty-six miles) three times weekly and Georgetown to Kokomo (connecting to Leadville) via Montezuma and Frisco, daily in Concord Coaches.*

GEORGETOWN

In the *Georgetown Courier*, March 6, 1879, there appeared the following notice:

> *S. W. Nott started a passenger and express line from Georgetown to Kokomo, which for the present will be run tri-weekly. Teams*

will leave Georgetown on Mondays, Wednesdays, and Fridays, and returning on Tuesdays, Thursdays, and Saturdays. Travel on this road is increasing and we presume it will not be a great while before a daily line will be established.

However, the winter of 1880-1881 was a most severe one in Georgetown. Numerous storms occurred, and abundant snow fell upon the range. The severe weather did not, however, stop the coaches. *The Georgetown Courier,* November 25, 1880, reported the following:

Nott's coaches go out loaded with passengers, baggage and express matter every morning. Notwithstanding, the usually stormy weather of this season, the trips have been made with regularity and safety, which speaks well for the management of the line and carefulness of the drivers.

The McLaughlin stage arrives at Peart's Ranch with a party who have come to celebrate a birthday country-style.

Courtesy of South Park City Collection

CHAPTER 12: NORTHWEST COLORADO

At the first station located on the way out of Georgetown — a mere twelve miles out — the stagecoach line reverted to sleighs. The sleighs had shoe-like brakes to keep them from going too fast down steep slopes.

Often, just before they reached a summit, horses were allowed a short breathing spell, then, after a few minutes, they made fast tracks down the other side. The drivers were dressed in heavy overcoats and caps — their feet wrapped with burlap. Sometimes, it would take three men to keep the road open by shoveling snow, so that the stagecoach could continue on its route.

GLENWOOD SPRINGS

As a general rule, the best recollections of historical events are those recorded in a diary or journal. The diary of Judge Arthur Livingston Beardsley was one of those. Judge Beardsley pursued the study of law in the office of the late John Kinkaid at Tin Cup, Gunnison, and Aspen. He practiced law in Glenwood Springs in February of 1887 and later moved to New Castle. A few entries in Judge Beardsley's diary tell some of the story of his travels in those times:

> Dec.1, 1886 — To Tincup today on Western Stageline at 8 a.m.
>
> Dec.2, 1886 — I left Tincup on the stage at noon. Dinner at Red Mountain. Aspen at 7 p.m, Supper at La Veta, stayed in a room over the furniture store.
>
> Dec. 25, 1886 — Christmas. Spent quietly. Dinner with Johnson at Mr. Beviens
>
> Jan. 1, 1887 — The most lonesome I have ever been.
>
> Feb.2, 1887 — Up before six. Breakfast at the La Veta. Took Stage at the Clarendon. Left Aspen a little after seven with eleven passengers, one school girl, eight went clear through with the addition of one who got on at Carbondale. Arrived at Glenwood at 4 p.m. Very windy and cold riding in the open sleigh in the morning, more comfortable in that respect as well as uncomfortable in respect to being very crowded in the coach but we proceeded so snail slow and were bumped so much that I became very tired.

In *The Glenwood Springs Ute Chief*, August 13, 1887, a news item appeared in regard to a stagecoach mishap:

> Apparently the uncoupling of the reach on the coach caused the stage accident with the coach and passengers on Tuesday evening,

while the stage was in rapid motion. Henderson, the driver, was thrown violently to the ground sustaining painful injuries while the horses ran. Dr. Hewitt is seriously injured about thigh and hip and cannot use his limb at all.

Although he is doing well now, he is under good medical and surgical attendance. Mr. Pelton of Sands, Pelton, and Company, was also hurt and is doing well with good attendance. He is also being cared for by Mr. Albert Morris. Mr. Arthur Seller was slightly hurt; Mr. Russell had his arm broken. This is the extent of the injuries sustained by the unfortunate accident and all are recovering nicely.

GRANBY

Prominent men in Granby during the 1890s were Charles H. Nuckolls, Laurence M. Tovey, Charles Lake, and R.J. Weston. Mr. Nuckolls, along with his wife, Sarah, operated the principal hotel, called the James Peak, where thirty-five cents bought guests an unlimited amount of food and people could cut loose on the second floor dance hall.

Mr. Tovey ran a stageline to Grand Lake and participated in Democratic politics. He was a man of little formal education but was intelligent and likable. He was thin, blue-eyed, and ruddy in the best Irish-American fashion. Mr. Lake ran a horseshoeing business and was also a barkeep, while Mr. Weston was the proprietor of a large-scale livery and feed stable.

GRAND LAKE

The community of Grand Lake in June of 1879 had six buildings; three on the west shore belonging to Judge Wescott, and cabins built on the north, the northwest, and the east shore. By fall of that year, a small store was built, as was the Grand Lake House. This hotel offered spring beds, mattresses, and a dining room that seated seventy-five people. Its Canadian-born owner, Wilson Walden, was active in the community and controlled interests in mines, ranches, livestock, and real estate. He brought with him to Grand Lake his wife, Eleanor, who was from the Isle of Man.

Other hotels appeared as early as 1881. The Garrison House and the Fairview House were located at the west end of the lake; stage travel under favorable conditions could result in a beautiful journey, but more often than not, it was tedious and uncomfortable.

A notable stop on the stage road to Grand Lake was the Lehman Ranch, which now lies at the bottom of the Granby Reservoir. In the 1890s, it was one of the earliest dude ranches in Colorado. The Johnson Ranch, located nearby, was also a stage stop. Upon reaching Grand Lake, one could stay at

A photo of Fred D. McLaren in his younger days. Mr. McLaren was a stagecoach driver for a time with the Tovey Stage Line that ran from Georgetown to Middle Park.
Courtesy of
Martha Boehner

the Kauffman House. The Grand Lake Historical Society has preserved this hotel, now renovated as a museum.

GRAND JUNCTION

Mesa County first began to be settled in the fall of 1881. Grand Junction was platted in 1882, and Mesa County became even larger when it took in part of Gunnison County in 1883.

Henry Rustler Rhone, the organizer and builder of the Roan Creek Toll Road, arrived in the newly organized town of Grand Junction after graduating from the Union College of Law in Chicago, Illinois. Rhone served as the City Attorney of Grand Junction and became active in civic affairs.

Rhone had a grand idea to build a toll road through Hogback Canyon. He felt it would open and enlarge the market area of Mesa County. His first attempt to convince some of his business friends of this moneymaking opportunity failed. But being a determined man, he tried again in 1884, finally quitting his job as City Attorney so that he could devote more time and attention to his dream. At last, after finally winning over his investors, the Roan Toll Road was built.

With the new road open, stagelines began regular service from Grand Junction to Glenwood Springs. The firm of Hammond and Kennedy advertised regular weekly stagecoach trips to Glenwood Springs. Another stageline, Prairie's Stage Company, began operation in 1888. An

View of men and a stagecoach in Grand Junction, Mesa County, Colorado; the Brunswick Hotel is a brick building with storefronts and a mansard roof. 1889

Courtesy of Denver Public Library, Western History Collection

advertisement proclaimed the time for reaching New Castle to be a mere eighteen hours — all for a fare of just eight dollars.

Today, DeBeque Canyon runs between the towns of Palisade and DeBeque. On the south side of the Colorado River is a paved highway. Along the north bank of the river, where stagecoaches once traveled, diesel-powered freight and passenger trains now make their way back and forth. If a modern day traveler looks carefully when passing through the canyon, remnants of Henry Rhone's old toll road are still visible.

HAYDEN

In a publication named *Three-Wire Winter, Inc, Vol. III, No.4, Issue #12*, one can find the story of the Dorey Family of Hayden, Colorado, as written by Jerry Green:

> *The Dorey family, Sherman, Estella, and their three daughters left for Colorado on October 17, 1911 via the railroad. Upon arrival at Steamboat Springs, they transferred to a stagecoach for the last leg of their trip. The girls were scared of the rocking, noisy coach pulled by four horses, so they sang all the way to Hayden.*

After their arrival in Hayden, Mr. Sherman engaged in the carpentry business doing framing, furniture repair, cabinet and carpenter work. In 1912 he was also in the undertaking and funeral direction profession.

HOT SULPHUR SPRINGS

The stage time in the summer of 1884 from Hot Sulphur Springs to Georgetown was usually twelve hours. Horses were frequently changed at McQuery's 4-Bar-4, which bypassed the Junction Ranch.

John A. Coulter, a former Georgetown attorney, was a shareholder in the Berthoud Pass-Hot Sulphur Springs Stage Road, and he built Coulter Stage Stop. In 1884, it became a post office and continued to serve the community until 1905. Near present-day U.S. Highway 40 were the stage stations of Barney Day and the King Ranches, where travelers of that era could stop for rest and food.

JEFFERSON

Mr. Willard Heal laid out the original town site of Jefferson in 1880. Mr. Heal, the first resident of Jefferson, eventually opened a store there and converted his house into a hotel and stage stop. He was also an early-day Park County Commissioner.

LEADVILLE

Spottswood and McClellan's stagelines, including the Denver and South Park Stage Line became active in the high mountains of Colorado as early as 1865. In 1877, the Federal Government advertised that a mail contract was to be allotted to Leadville. Spottswood hurried to Washington, D.C. as soon as he heard the word and bought the franchise. In 1877, they completed their line over the mountain to Leadville. They originally considered the route over Mosquito Pass, but rejected it and chose a longer route until the road was improved in 1879.

In early day Leadville, one of the first stageline customers happened to be a young man from Holland, John J. Vandemoer. Mr. Vandemoer left Denver by rail in early spring, and, when he reached Morrison, he boarded one of Spottswood and McClellan's stages on his way to Fairplay. After traveling a day and a night, he finally reached his destination. Mr. Vandemoer decided to stay in Fairplay to rest up from the tiring journey.

The next morning, he took the stage on over to Leadville. While it was early spring in Denver, on Weston Pass it was still midwinter. The snow was six feet deep, and it was extremely cold. As they approached the Leadville side of the mountain, they encountered a group of traveling musicians who had slipped down the side of the mountain — wagon, horses, and all. The stage passengers checked to see if anyone was injured, then helped them get back on the road. Only one violin had been broken, so the extent of damage was minimal due to the soft snow, which apparently had cushioned their descent.

The stage driver promised to send help as soon as they arrived in Leadville. Around 3 a.m., they reached the Arkansas River about seven miles below Leadville, and from there they followed the frozen stream's left bank until they reached the Magic City.

The most common route into Leadville from the east was Weston Pass. However, when extremely heavy snow hampered their travel, they had to go further south to Trout Creek Pass. Barlow and Sanderson and Wall and Witter owned stagelines that traveled in and out of Leadville.

MARBLE

Before the turn of the century, The Crystal River Stageline provided passenger and express service in and out of the town of Marble. The stage provided the town's only real link with civilization before the advent of the railroad, leaving from Crystal and Carbondale daily — except on Sundays.

The winter of 1898-1899 was so severe that even the Crystal River Railway Company had to discontinue work on building their line until the following spring. The Denver Post printed the following letter from Crystal:

> Crystal is snowbound! The stage road between this city and Marble, six miles below, is under from ten to fifty feet of snow and the mail carrier has only been able to come through once in the past week and then on snowshoes. Supplies will be exhausted in a short time, and unless the road can be opened up, several mines will probably be forced to close down and the miners go out on snowshoes.
>
> As soon as the storm has ceased and the weather settles, a force of fifty men will begin work to open the road for a train of pack horses to bring in supplies and it is believed that by tunneling through the snow at points most exposed to avalanches it will be possible to open a trail long enough to bring in supplies.

An interesting fact is that Marble was granted a contract to furnish the stone to be used in the interior of the Colorado State Capital Building in 1895. 140,000 square feet of marble was needed for the Capital project — an extraordinary amount for that time.

This old stagecoach is being restored by the Silt Historical Society.
It originally ran from Rifle to Meeker and was owned by the Harp
Transportation Line.

Courtesy of Silt Historical Society

MEEKER

According to *Crofutt's Grip-Sack Guide of 1885,* "Meeker, in Garfield County, formerly known as the White River Indian Agency, is situated in Agency Park, on the White River, 161 miles south of Rawlins, Wyo. It is connected (to Denver) by stagecoach requiring 45 hours time to reach Meeker. Population is about 200, most of whom are ranchers and stockmen."

Mr. A.E. Rees and son purchased the Harp Transportation Line from Uncle Horace Simpson Harp in the spring of 1905. They took over the operation of the business, which included livery stables in Rifle and Meeker, two Concord stagecoaches, between thirty and forty teams of horses, other miscellaneous rolling equipment, and two swing stations. The line carried all the U.S. mail to and from Meeker, going as far north as Craig and providing passenger service to Meeker and to Axial Basin by way of Nine Mile Hill. It also provided express and freight service to the White River Valley. The stage carried passengers along the Government Road, stopping at Piciance Creek for dinner.

RANGELY

The first white settlers in the Rangely area after the eviction of the Ute

Indians in 1881 were Charles P. Hill and Joseph Studer. They arrived in 1882 with a herd of cattle and followed by an array of settlers.

At the turn of the century, the Goff Trading Post was built down the White River, west of Rangely. A stageline served the trading post, and another road, following old Indian trails down the river into Utah, was also built.

There are still visible signs of stage stops along the river, usually where a ford is located. If you know where to look, one can still find the foundation stones. There were apparently several stops where stage passengers, cattlemen, sheepmen, and traders could spend the night.

One stagecoach stop in Rangely is close to where the original settlement of the town occurred, just east of where the town is presently located.

SILVER PLUME

In 1885, Silver Plume was a lively mining camp resting two miles above Georgetown, near the many mines at the base of the Sherman and Republican Mountains. Daily mail and passenger stagecoaches ran from Silver Plume to Georgetown at regular intervals during the day and evening. The population was somewhere around 600 people.

STEAMBOAT SPRINGS

The firm of Whipple and Stafford was the first stageline established for carrying passengers to Steamboat Springs. A.J. Stafford, the first partner of D.W. Whipple in the stage business, was killed in a runaway accident when he was driving on Riley Wilson Hill near Phippsburg. There were several passengers on the stage but no one else was hurt.

When spring finally arrived, the coaches could only travel at night, when the snow was frozen on the trails. When half a dozen early railroads of the state were halted because of snow, the Steamboat-Wolcott Stage still made it through every night. If one stage did not arrive on time, another would be sent out to search for the missing one. Sometimes, there were eight or nine stagecoaches on the road at the same time, trying to reach the stage that was stranded.

D.W. Whipple's four Concord stagecoaches could hold fifteen passengers, with nine people residing inside the coach and six more up on the roof. The Rock Creek Stage Station on Gore Pass was added to the National Register of Historic Places in 1982.

CHAPTER THIRTEEN

CITIES AND TOWNS ALONG THE TRAIL: SOUTHWEST COLORADO

C olorado, west of the Continental Divide, belonged to Mexico until 1848, when it was ceded to the United States following the Mexican War. The Continental Divide is a jagged ridge that runs southwest through the state. It is from high in the Rocky Mountains that the major rivers of Colorado originate. From peaks towering over 14,000 feet in elevation, spring the waters of the Platte, the San Juan, the Rio Grande, and the great rapids of the Arkansas and Colorado Rivers.

Mining in the San Juan Mountain area of Southwestern Colorado grew slowly but steadily in the 1870s. This was Colorado's silver era, with mining camps springing up all across the mountain ranges. Mines in legendary places like Ouray and Silverton made millions of dollars for those willing to take a chance, turning many ordinary men into millionaires.

When gold and silver were discovered in the San Juans, Barlow and Sanderson concentrated their efforts on expanding their routes in this area. In June 1870, the stage company had acquired contracts to carry the U.S. Mail in the Colorado Territory. A month later, Barlow and Sanderson bought the Denver and Santa Fe Stageline as a subsidiary, renaming it the "Southern Overland Mail and Express." Soon, Barlow and Sanderson became the largest stageline in all of Colorado.

ALAMOSA

The town of Alamosa was laid out in June of 1878, and the railroad reached the town later that month. Situated on the west bank of the Rio Grande River, Alamosa sat almost in the center of the San Luis Valley.

By 1878, Alamosa had one bank and a large variety of stores that carried large supplies of goods. The Palmer and the Victoria were the principal hotels, and there were churches of various denominations.

The Perry House was the terminal of Barlow and Sanderson's Stageline in the newly formed town of Alamosa. Stages were routed northwestward from Del Norte to Saguache, Barnum, and Ouray; westward to Del Norte and Lake City; southward to Santa Fe; and southwestward to Alamosa, Conejos, and Santa Fe.

As the product of a lively, southwestern town, Alamosa's stagecoaches hauled an enormous amount of merchandise and machinery daily for the San Juan mining region and Gunnison County.

ALMONT

Ten miles north of Gunnison and sixteen miles south of Crested Butte was the little settlement of Almont. At this point, the Taylor River met the Gunnison to form the larger and more beautiful Gunnsion River. The small settlement became an important location because of the railroad that carried the famous Doctor Mine ore from Crested Butte in 1879.

Sam Fisher built a toll road across the Taylor River, as well as a road to the mouth of Spring Creek. The early town was named "Fisher" after Sam Fisher, but, after a time, he renamed it "Almont," after a famous horse known as the leading Hambletonian Stallion of that century.

Before long, Almont acquired a U.S. Post Office and a railroad depot. But more importantly, it became a gathering place for settlers and miners of the region. When the big rush came to Gunnison County in 1879-1881, Sam Fisher became a very wealthy man. Barlow and Sanderson ran two daily stages through Almont in 1881; additionally, as many as five hundred travelers made their way past the junction every week.

And yet, it seems, all good things must eventually come to an end. Sam Fisher's toll road ceased operation between the Gunnison River and Jack's Cabin in 1881, when the Denver and Rio Grande Railroad ran a twenty-eight mile branch line to Crested Butte. In 1883, Gunnison County officials purchased the old toll road for a county road.

BUENA VISTA

A fascinating book entitled, *Buena Vista, Tales of the Past,* colorfully written by Suzy Kelly, points out that:

There were busy stagelines operating in the valley before rail-roads arrived. Barlow and Sanderson's Overland Stage was one of the major lines. It operated ten or more coaches a day between Leadville and Cañon City. This is the stagecoach road you can see north of Buena Vista on the East Side of the Arkansas River. There is a sign pointing to the road from Highway 24.

Joe Hawkins and Skinny Pyle often drove the stagecoach from Buena Vista to St. Elmo over Tin Cup Pass. Ed Vickers was another driver for the stage in the winter, when a sleigh was generally used in order to combat snowdrifts twenty-feet deep.

If one climbs to the top of Mt. Princeton and knows what to look for, faint tracks are still visible of the old stage and freight roads into Buena Vista.

CIMARRON

In 1875, Cimarron was known as Cline's Ranch, where an old toll road brought stages and traffic to the small settlement. Otto Mears was most responsible for the roads in and out of Gunnison Country. He received a contract to carry supplies to the Utes and was awarded a government contract to carry the mail from Lake City to Ouray by way of the Uncompahgre Agency. Mears built the road in 1875-76. The new route originated at the junction of the Saguache and San Juan Road near Barnum on the Lake Fork of the Gunnison River and climbed steeply to reach Blue Mesa. The road traveled across the mesa for several miles, through what is now property that belongs to the Ute Tribe, and descended near Halfway House. The trail followed a route along today's Highway 50 for about nine miles. The toll road then headed west from the point where Cimarron Creek and the Little Cimarron join, finally coming into the settlement of Cimarron.

CEDAREDGE

In Cedaredge, located in the eastern section of the Uncompahgre Valley, the first blacksmith shop was built by George Leason. J.L. Vanaken also operated a shop in the northwest corner of the town. The first livery barn, built by Bob James for Sam Lovett, was a colorful building with a picture of an elk painted on the front. This undoubtedly was the first "mural" painted in Delta County.

Sam Lovett had been working for the Bar I Ranch when he built his own house in Cedaredge. He worked at the livery barn and also drove a stagecoach to Delta to deliver mail and passengers to the U.S. Post Office. His wife was manager of the Post Office at that time. A few of the other stagecoach drivers in Cedaredge at the time were men by the name of Elliot, "Dad" Lambert, and Holly Miller, who drove for several years.

CREEDE

In discussing western towns, one must not forget the town of Creede, which was one of the last great silver camps in 1890. When silver was discovered nearby, some 10,000 excited prospectors eagerly made Creede their home. The first settlement there was named "Jimtown," but, because of the excessive amount of saloons, the name was changed to "Gintown." About 1891, the town finally named itself after its founding father. At that time, there were over thirty saloons and a variety of stores and hotels.

At the turnoff for Clear Creek Falls, located between Lake City and Creede, is a sign with the following information:

> *This is the route of the Antelope Park-Lake City Toll Road. It was built in 1875 at a cost of $5000.00 and was completed for wagon travel in less than sixty days. The route was used by the*

The Antelope Park/Lake City toll road was built in 1875 after the discovery of gold in the region. Barlow & Sanderson's Stage Co. had way stations located twelve miles apart. The stage took thirty-six hours to travel the 85 mile route. The Belford Stage Station wass located to the north of Clear Creek Falls. Stage hands replaced horses and repaired coaches and harnesses while passengers were offered food, overnight lodging, and a view of Clear Creek Falls.

Author's Photo Collection

Barlow and Sanderson Stagecoach Company, which had way stations, located twelve miles apart. The stage took thirty-six hours to travel the 85-mile route between Del Norte and Lake City. The fare was $16.50 per person. The Belford Stage Station was located to the north of Clear Creek Falls. Stagehands replaced horses and repaired coaches and harnesses while passengers were offered food and overnight lodging, and a view of the Clear Creek Falls. Infrequently used after 1885, when the Denver and Rio Grande Railroad arrived in Gunnison, this road received a new lease on life in the 1890s, when silver was discovered near Creede. Miners used this route to return to Creede from Lake City.

CRESTED BUTTE

In August of 1880, Crested Butte boasted a population of 400, with another 1,000 miners living within a three-mile radius of the town. The first mayor of Crested Butte was a man named Howard Smith. The new town of Crested Butte had fifty businesses, dwellings and tents, a smelter, three sawmills, and a fine hotel named the "Forest Queen." This elegant hotel was situated amidst the splendor of the Elk Mountains, which towered in the background.

Transportation to and from Crested Butte was a huge challenge, as heavy snow, bitter cold, and isolation hampered the efforts. However, in 1880, the Pioneer Toll Road joined Crested Butte to the booming silver camp of Irwin, nine miles to the west. The same summer, a rough trail was constructed between Gunnison and Crested Butte. This allowed the Barlow and Sanderson's Stagelines access into the "Gateway of the Elks." In the fall of 1881, another toll road was built, and it was named the "Crested Butte, Ashcroft, and Gothic Toll Road." In the meantime, across the Elk Mountains to the north, Aspen and Ashcroft were desperately trying to get their ore to the railroad in Crested Butte. Although primitive roads were built over east Maroon Pass and Pearl Pass during the 1880s, efforts to keep them open year-round failed. The extremely steep grades, violent snowstorms, and heavy spring and summer rains were the cause of the failure.

During the 1880s, Crested Butte was an important transportation and supply center — despite the weather — as shown on the streets of the small town, where could be seen hundreds of braying burros waiting to be loaded with supplies for the surrounding mining camps.

DEL NORTE

Del Norte was established in 1872 on the western side of the San Luis Valley. The little town was considered the "Gateway to the San Juans," and was a supply base for miners and freighters heading toward the San Juan Mountains. Along with the wagons carrying freight, stagecoaches brought mail, express, and passengers from Pueblo and Cucharis to Del Norte.

Hopes ran high in the spring of 1875 for an extension of Barlow and Sanderson's stage service to the San Juan mines. Jared L. Sanderson, the active partner in the stageline, arrived in Del Norte in June to establish it. Sanderson said that, if a road to the Animas District was not built, the Barlow and Sanderson service between Cañon City and Del Norte would be reduced to tri-weekly runs. Brewster's stageline served the Stoney Pass route, handling both freight and passengers.

Jesse Scarff was born in 1883 and shared in a 1972 interview much of what she had apparently been told by her mother about the Barlow and Sanderson stagecoaching operation. The Scarff family lived in the two-room log cabin directly north across from Lookout Hill on the west edge of Del Norte.

> There was the stage barn on the Barlow and Sanderson lot, which has a long barn from the alley to the street. The stage driver threw down his line; he was through with his work for the day. The driver made those horses go like nobody's business, they didn't just let them trot along. Barlow and Sanderson didn't buy cheap horses. As soon as the stagecoach drove into the lot, the tenders would put the horses into the barn as soon as they could because the horses were just steaming; the drivers drove them so fast. The tenders put two horses into each manger and blanketed them. They didn't feed them for an hour. The tenders would let the horses stand and in an hour would take off the blankets. Then the horses were rubbed and curried until they fairly shone. Forty some head of horses were pastured in the area to keep the stages rolling.
>
> The Barlow and Sanderson coaches were the most beautiful, great big Concord coaches. They were black, very black, with shiny gold mountings on them. I think it was eight passengers could ride the inside of those big coaches. The coaches had things fixed around frames to hold the baggage. People who didn't want to pay full fare could ride on the boot if they wished but they hardly every rode there; when snow came it was very, very bad. There were six horses to those big coaches, and they were beautifully matched horses.

The Barlow and Sanderson Stage Station was located on the west end of Del Norte at 220 Grande Avenue, on the north side of the road and opposite the base of Mount Lookout. The station was approximately 15 x 20 feet, and it was built of hand-hewn, red spruce logs. The building was held together with square nails, and sported a dirt or gable roof, two windows on the east wall, and a door on the south wall. This was the same layout in nearly all the other stage stations in the valley.

LA POSTA

Located about fourteen miles south of Durango on 213 Road was the little village of La Posta, which means "Stage Station." It was originally a stage-coach stop and post office on the way to Farmington, New Mexico, and Durango. The tiny village was established in May of 1899 during the land rush on the Ute strip, in which part of the Indian reservation had been opened to homesteaders.

GUNNISON

Gunnison County's claim to fame is its great, clear trout streams, fine cattle ranches, lush mountain ranges, and wonderful summer climate. The past, however, holds the rich historic prosperity of this region, which was as famous for its drama, adventure, and legends as any part of the West.

During the early spring months of 1880, all roads led into Gunnison, which was transformed from an isolated sagebrush settlement with only a

View of the La Veta Hotel, 219 S. Boulevard, Gunnison, (Gunnison County), Colorado; shows a Victorian brick structure with mansard roofs and dormers. Stagecoaches and buggies are at the entry; cliffs and hills are in the background.

Courtesy of Colorado Historical Society

Photos of the old Otto Mears stagecoach trail over Blue Mesa in Gunnison County, Colorado.

Author's Collection

few log huts and tents to a roaring boomtown overnight. Gunnison had a population of about 25,000 people during the rush of 1880.

Stagecoaching in the Gunnison area was a story all its own. Early-day stagecoaches traveling to and from Gunnison often had nine or ten passengers squeezed into seats designed for six. One lady passenger who came in on a Barlow and Sanderson stage in 1880 exclaimed that she "didn't know what scared her most, the fear of an Indian attack or going back over Marshall Pass."

The stagelines would have to change horses five times between Gunnison and the Arkansas River, using four horses for the first three changes and six on the last two. A stage into Lake City in 1882 was comprised of a six-horse team, made up of white or dappled-gray horses.

Gunnison was a social hub in July 1880, when Barlow and Sanderson extended the stageline to run a twice daily line of four-horse stagecoaches from Salida to Gunnison and Pitkin. This line carried General Ulysses S. Grant and his party when the famous persona visited the region.

HOTCHKISS/CRAWFORD

One of the most impressive entrepreneurs among Hotchkiss's early pioneers was John Edward Hanson, a native of Denmark. In 1881, he first

Stagecoach that served Paonia, Delta, and Hotchkiss, Colorado 1890
Courtesy of Colorado Historical Society

arrived in Colorado from Michigan, where his family home was located. Hanson worked for the Denver and Rio Grande Railroad as it built its narrow gauge line over Marshall Pass. He also filed for and received a quarter section of land at Parlin, near Gunnison.

In 1883, while visiting a friend, Joseph Reich of Hotchkiss, the opportunity arose for Hanson to move there and help Joseph operate the North Fork mail route. The mail route ran twice a week and included a freight/passenger hauling business. Ed Hanson went into business with Joseph after they landed the contract to haul mail back and forth between Paonia and Delta. They purchased a stagecoach, and a four-horse team to pull it, and were soon hauling passengers, freight, and mail. The business continued until Ed Hanson sold his interest to Joseph Reich in 1886.

LA JARA

The tiny town of La Jara was settled in the 1870s, but not incorporated until 1895. It was a busy marketing and supply center for the railroad and various other enterprises.

William A. Braiden, a native of Ohio, arrived in Conejos County in 1887, trailing a herd of shorthorn cattle. He sold his herd and went to work for dairy farmers and ranchers in the area until he had enough money to start his own herd of horses. He owned and operated the Pioneer Livery Barn in La Jara, became a livestock dealer, owned a retail store, had businesses in Creede, and operated the stageline.

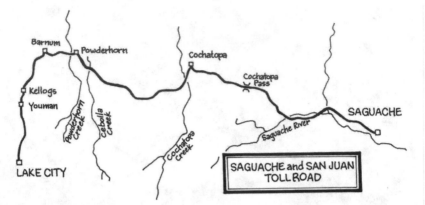

Sketch of a map of the Lake City, Colorado, area, including Saguache and the San Juan Toll road.

Sketch by Steven M. Burke

LAKE CITY

Lake City was an important stagecoach town in the 1870s. It was the terminus of the Antelope Springs and Lake City Toll Road and the Saguache and San Juan Toll Road, giving it two outlets to the east and one wagon road over Engineer Pass to the mines beyond the range. Barlow and Sanderson's Overland Stageline made tri-weekly trips from Cañon City to Lake City, carrying mail and passengers.

Lake City quickly grew to have five general stores, two bakeries, two blacksmith shops, two sawmills, three restaurants, one livery stable, and a weekly newspaper, *The Silver World*. The population reached a peak of 2,500 residents in 1877 before beginning to decline.

Lake City was the only town of importance in Hinsdale County. There were other settlements along the stage road up Engineer and Cinnamon Passes, but these were very small camps.

In the summer of 1877, *The Silver World* wrote:

> *In 1877 property advanced rapidly in value; lots which on the first of December, or January, could not find purchasers at $250-$300, by the first of March commanded $500-600. Buildings went up like magic. So great was the supply for lumber that the mills could not supply the demand.*

At the beginning of the year, the coaches were coming into Lake City loaded with passengers, compelling the stageline to begin offering daily service. By April, coaches coming into the town were bulging with passengers, and they just kept coming.

MONTROSE

This small settlement was incorporated in 1882, growing from a few sod shacks and log cabins to more permanent brick buildings and businesses — gradually becoming a thriving and diverse community.

By 1883, Montrose was beginning to have a "downtown." The businesses included a post office, a newspaper, a grocery store, a hardware store, a Chinese laundry, and a little "café." As the need for a hotel emerged, Otto Mears, the famous toll road and railroad builder, and Joseph Selig erected a two-story palace-type building on the corner of Main and Cascade. The rooms had canvas partitions, and the downstairs bar was filled with every gambling device that had ever been invented.

It was the fourteen saloons that provided the revenue for the new town. Saloons were taxed a hundred dollars a year, to be paid at the little frame courthouse on Main Street.

The "Carriage Works" building. It has been rebuilt on the east edge of Montrose by Richard E. Fike, the executive director of the Museum of the Mountain West, Inc.

Three stagecoach lines had daily service from the Mears Hotel, which later was known as "Lott's Hotel." Two factories were built in order to supply the bricks for downtown buildings, and native rock was quarried from surrounding hillsides. Because of the increasing development, transportation in the Montrose area continued to progress.

In 1882, a very poor dirt wagon road was built into the Uncompahgre Valley from the east. It ran from Lake City via Pine Creek Cutoff, across Blue Mesa, down a very steep road known as "Son-of-a-Gun Hill," and into Blue Creek Canyon.

Montrose had a noteworthy building called the "Carriage Works." The enterprise thrived as Montrose's demand increased for brand-specific parts and repairs for horse-drawn carriages and stagecoaches traveling through the region. Anyone needing a horse shod, carriage repaired, or a new Studebaker wagon to buy found it at Montrose's Carriage Works. The old building stood for many years before recently being torn down to make room for more development. The good news is that, on another site, it is being rebuilt using the original lumber, which had been numbered for easy reconstruction.

Men and boys are on top of and in a stagecoach drawn by a team of four horses in front of the Dallas Hotel and Saloon, Dallas, Ouray County, Colorado. People are on the balcony of the two-story hotel and along the boardwalk in front of the wood frame buildings. Large block letters are painted on the wood shingle roof, "Dallas Saloon," and on the false front, "Dallas Hotel." 1880

Courtesy of Denver Public Library, Western History Collection

OURAY

Dave Wood, the well-known freighter, told the following story about stage-coaching in the late 1800s in a book, written by his two daughters, called *I Hauled These Mountains in Here.*

> After we made Montrose our home base for work into the mountains, I bought out the Great Western Stage Company and began a stageline into Ouray. This was a large, covered stage running both ways every day. It usually left Montrose each morning

The Ouray County Historical Museum has one of the largest collections of old photos of stagecoaches and the stagecoach era of any place in the state of Colorado, including this one of the Circle Route Stage on Red Mountain Pass.

with 25-27 passengers and a ton of express and baggage. The distance was 38 miles. Our first two changes in routes were 12 miles apart and we used teams of four large horses. The last route was 14 miles from Dallas, and we put on six-horses, nice, well-matched teams. The drivers were men thoroughly experienced in the work; one Lou Hill had driven a stage out of Chicago fifty years before, clear down into Tennessee. He had driven stages at various placers all the fifty years between, and his wife had kept stations for the drivers.

In an unpublished manuscript, Frank Rice tells of stagecoaching in Ouray:

In 1884, J. L. Sanderson and Company advertised that their coaches left Montrose for Ouray and Telluride at 2 p.m. No time of arrival was specified. Horses were changed at the Halfway House. Somewhat altered, the house still stands — the first one north of Cow Creek on the east side of Highway 550.

An echo of the past, Ouray, Colorado, September 16, 1923.
Courtesy of Colorado Historical Society

The Circle Route stage is just departing from Ouray in front of the Beaumont Hotel about 1895. It is being pulled by six large and powerful horses, which they will definitely need to pull the stagecoach over Red Mountain Pass.

Courtesy of P. David Smith

It is a pity that not one of the old time stagecoaches and busses remains in Ouray. All were traded or given away with no thought of the future historical value. The "Pioneer Stage" driven in parades at Norwood could be one of our hotel busses — at least the design is the same. Both the Beaumont and Western Hotels used a horse drawn bus to carry passengers to and from trains. Standing side-by-side at the depot, each driver loudly extolled the merits of his hostelry. Passengers between Ouray and Red Mountain rode in Concord coaches of the same design as those used on the pioneer runs across the prairies. Drawn by four or six horses, a driver and one favored passenger rode on the outer front seat. Mail and baggage were carried in the boot at the rear. Other passengers rode inside the enclosed body of the stage. From construction of the Mears Toll Road in 1881 until 1910, all travelers over the road were carried in the same Concord coaches. Dan Cutshall and Art Stewart were two well-known drivers of the day; Stewart quit the

The Riverside snow tunnel high up on the Ouray Toll Road, Ouray County, Colorado.

Courtesy of P. David Smith

old Beaumont Livery Co., but left the business to employees while he gave personal attention to the stage.

Snow was the enemy of the Colorado stagecoach! At the first sign of a freeze, blacksmith shops would be jammed with stock, all waiting to be shod with cleats. Sleigh runners replaced wheels and, on steep downgrades,

Snow not only caused problems when it fell, but also when it melted. The fifty-foot high bridge on the Silverton Toll Road crossed Red Mountain Creek. The bridge was several times washed away by floods (some debris from previous floods is underneath the bridge in the canyon).

Courtesy of P. David Smith

Circle Route Stage high up on Red Mountain Pass with a well-dressed passenger.

Courtesy of P. David Smith

A large, well-dressed group sitting on a stagecoach for a portrait on Red Mountain Pass. One wonders if this small coach could haul this many passengers up such a steep mountain grade.

Courtesy of
P. David Smith

the runners were rough-locked with chains; additional braking was some-times furnished by dragging an anchor-like claw or large logs, which con-tributed to the rough and torn-up nature of the roads.

Ike Stephens, driving the stage from Ouray over Red Mountain with a big load of eggs, dead pigs, general merchandise, and two hung-over min-ers, had his horses get scared and run away. The horses pulled Ike free, but all of his freight — including the sleeping miners — shot over the cliff like they were fired from a Cañon, dropped a hundred feet or so to a steep slope, and skidded to a tangled mess in the creek below. The eggs were gone, the pigs already dead, the merchandise ruined, but somehow the miners were fished out still alive and breathing.

Even animals wore snowshoes occasionally. Flat boards were bolted to their hoofs and equipped with sharp cleats to prevent slipping. When a real emergency arose, a man might put his own wool socks on a horse's front feet to enable it to get better traction on ice, or smear butter over its hoofs to help keep snow from balling them up into crippling masses.

In the winter months, crews were constantly shoveling out snowslides, but one winter, the Riverside Slide between Ouray and Silverton spilled too much snow across the highway for workers to remove. A temporary road was built over the snowslide, but spring thaws softened the surface snow into an impassable and unsafe slush. Accordingly, Otto Mears bored a 580-foot long snow tunnel through the slide, making it high enough to pass a six-horse Concord stage. The tunnel lasted well into the summer and became a source of pride to the natives, who appreciated its secondary function as a unique tourist attraction.

PAGOSA SPRINGS

The stage to and from New Mexico left Pagosa Springs going south over what is now Highway 84, about twelve miles to what was then called the "Halfway House" at Spiler or Halfway Canyon, then continued on its way to Price (now called "Chromo") about twenty-four miles south of Pagosa Springs.

The stage to and from Durango (then called "Animas City") left Pagosa Springs heading west. There was a stage stop located about twelve miles out from Pagosa Springs en route past the Piedra River. The stop was called the "Peterson Stage Station." There, passengers could get meals and a place to stay overnight. From that point, the stage continued on over Yellow Jacket toward the Pine River (now Bayfield), and on into Animas City.

The following article appeared in the *Pagosa Progress*, May 1977:

We pass it often, the stately structure setting back of U.S. Highway 160 near the Piedra River Bridge. We know the building has a history, but few of us have taken the moments needed to find out why the fading words, "Rocky Mountain," were painted across the front.

On the other side of the highway lives a man named Wayne Farrow. In 1879, the Farrow family homesteaded here and bought out the rights to 160 acres. Nearby, about 1890, this building was constructed on the old stage road. John Peterson owned it then; he employed a housekeeper to live there and to feed and house the stageline passengers.

After the big flood of 1911, Wayne Farrow's father bought the unused roadhouse, numbered each log, and in 1934 moved the structure to its present location as a house for a hired hand.

Today, Vandy and Barbara Powell own the building. But what about the painted words, "Rocky Mountain?" Wayne Farrow's father was named "Rocky Mountain" by Wayne's part-Indian grandmother.

So the next time you cross the Piedra River Bridge, look for that old building behind the Chimney Rock Post Office and think about weary travelers climbing off a creaking stagecoach in the shadow of Devil Mountain, and a man aptly named "Rocky Mountain" Farrow. It's the history of our country.

PLACERVILLE

In the long ago days of the Telluride mining camps, the settlements of Ilium, Ames, Ophir, Trout, and Rico were the center of much activity along a rough and bumpy road paralleling today's highway. Sargents was a stage stop just west of where the Telluride road branched off. Further to the northwest was the small town of Placerville on the San Miguel River.

In the early 1880s, Placerville was a bustling center of placer mining, as well as being the first town on the rough dirt road that crossed Dallas Divide. There were freight and stage stations every twelve miles along the route.

POWDERHORN

In the summer of 1874, a Saguache businessmen's group planned to capture all of the trade going into the San Juan mining area from their rival town, Del Norte. They hired Enos Hotchkiss and Otto Mears to build a toll road from Saguache to the Animas Valley. The wagon road was to be 130 miles long, crossing over exceedingly rugged country in western Colorado. The Cebolla-Powderhorn Valley seemed to be the best route into Lake City and the San Juans, so the road was built through there.

In late July of 1874, the Saguache-San Juan Toll Road had extended its length to one hundred miles, reaching all the way to Lake San Cristobal by early August. However, it was not until July 11, 1875, that the Lake City newspaper, *The Silver World*, reported the arrival of the first stagecoach of the Barlow and Sanderson Stageline from Saguache. After this, tri-weekly trips between Lake City and Saguache carried mail and passengers, and several stage stations were set up along this route.

In 1875, John and Narcissa McDonough were some of the first settlers to come to the Powderhorn Valley. They lived in Saguache for five years before moving their family to the valley, where John ran a stage station and trading center for horses and other stock, which were in great demand along the route. The stage station was located near the junction of the Deldorita and Cebolla Creeks on what is now called the "Howard Ranch."

The Andrew Stone family arrived in this valley in 1876. They ran a hotel and stage stop for weary travelers along the toll road. The Cebolla Hot Springs was the site of the stage stop.

RICO

In 1879, the discovery of silver in this mining district by Colonel J.C. Haggerty brought hordes of prospectors. The name finally chosen for the little town was "Rico," meaning "Rich," after names like "Carbon City," "Carbonville," "Lead City," and "Dolores City" had been mulled over.

Rico was a busy town, a fact reflected by one's observation that Dave Wood's freighting outfits and Meserole and Blake's stagelines were usually full, both coming and going. George Barlow, who was trying to get his equipment to Rico in order to start a sawmill, got his wagons with his equipment stuck so often that one could find the sawmill strung out all the way from Placerville to Rico. He eventually managed to get it all together in one place and establish his business.

SAGUACHE

It is believed that the Eureka Hotel in Saguache was the first stage station in Saguache. H. Lueders operated as its agent. The next station, located just west of the town, was built in 1870-1871 by Samuel Hoagland and was known as "Hoagland's Station" or "Halfway House," because it was halfway between Saguache and the final approach to the divide between the San Luis and Arkansas Valleys. It was originally built as a stopover place for people traveling to Gunnison County over Cochetopa, or to the first Los Pinos Indian Agency (operated from 1868-1875). In 1875, when the Lake City toll road opened, Hoagland's was a Barlow and Sanderson home station with overnight facilities for passengers and horses.

After the stages quit running, it became a boarding house, serving meals and offering lodging. The building was also used much like a community house, and various civic groups held dances there. Road workers later boarded there and kept their stock in its stables.

The Saguache Current reported meeting General Ulysses S. Grant and visiting with him at the Saguache Hotel. General Grant stopped at Hoagland's Station on his way to see Bonanza City.

The remaining building of Hoagland's Stage Station can still be seen behind piles of road material left from the contractor who built the Cochetopa Pass Highway.

SARGENTS

On the western side of Marshall Pass was a small settlement originally called "Marshalltown." In 1882, the name of the town was changed to "Sargents" after Joseph Sargent, who had once worked for the Los Pinos Indian Agency and established his ranch there. When settlers began moving in, a post office was established, and Joseph Sargent became the postmaster.

The town of Sargents developed into a busy little burg when Barlow and Sanderson provided stage service from there to Gunnison and six freighting companies began doing business within its city limits, using Sargents as their base of operations.

SILVERTON

The only town in San Juan County presently (and the county seat) is Silverton. In 1885, the town was bustling with businesses of all kinds, including hotels, smelting and sampling works, chlorinating works, sawmills, schools, and churches. The altitude of the town is 9,200 ft., making it one of the highest in Colorado.

In 1884, because of the Red Mountain mining boom, a new wagon road was built between Silverton and Ouray. Silverton was a real boomtown. There were practically more mines at that time than there were people, and stages were constantly leaving for Ouray, Lake City, and Durango (Animas City).

TELLURIDE

According to Dave Wood, the well-known freighter of the day, Telluride had its share of problems with stagecoaching.

Part of the road to Telluride was covered with deep snow in the winter. The Stage Company was trying to operate its line to

Telluride with buckboards and horses. At the snow, I transferred my loads to big sleds. My teams with their sleds caught one of the buckboards stalled one day in deep snow, with no chance to get out. W. B. VanAtta, a prominent merchant of Telluride, and his wife and child were in it, in danger of perishing in the snow. Of course, my drivers took care of them and took them in to Netherly's where they had comfort, warmth and food.

TIN CUP

Tin Cup was as violent and high-rolling a town as ever existed in Gunnison County. Originally known as "Virginia City," the founders of the town had come from Deadwood, Lead, and Spearfish — the famous old gold towns of the Black Hills region in 1875-76. They were accustomed to using their six-shooters for settling any differences.

William Woll, a twenty-one year old man seeking his first adventure in the West, arrived in Virginia City in the spring of 1879 in a six-horse stage-coach. On one side of the main thoroughfare were tents, cabins made of hand-hewn logs, and a few made from real lumber. Lured from the east by tales of quick wealth and hidden treasure, he was determined not to return until he had realized his dreams.

Woll pitched his tent on a lot next to one of the saloons, and it nearly cost him his life. One night, shots rang out from the saloon. The young man stayed put and did not get up to investigate. When he woke in the morning, he was terrified to find eight bullet holes in his tent.

By 1884, enthusiasm and interest in mining was waning in Tin Cup. There were only a few producing mines left, and the payroll was beginning to shrink as well. Other mining towns such as Ruby Camp, Gothic, Tomichi, and Aspen had called away the wandering miners, filling their minds with hopes and dreams of finally making a big strike. In 1886, Tin Cup only had 400 residents left. The stage still ran daily through Aspen, but not many passengers stayed in Tin Cup. Times were changing!

WAGON WHEEL GAP

In the early 1870s, Wagon Wheel Gap was a busy stage station on the route from Del Norte to Lake City. In 1877, a hotel was built at the hot springs and mineral springs, and it flourished. The town was supposedly named for the discovery of a large wagon wheel left by the Baker prospecting party of 1861 on their way to the mountains. After that, it was always referred to as the "Gap."

CHAPTER FOURTEEN

THE FINAL STAGES

I t seems as if the stagecoach era has disappeared for all time. Some people think of it as simply being a dramatic aspect of frontier life, with
little or no relevance to today's social concerns. Some think it of as being
merely a mode of transportation preceding the railroad. But what would
have became of this country if it weren't for the grand Concord stagecoach?
What about the brave men who drove it, and the people with foresight to
build it, making it the grandest vehicle of its day?

With the Railroad Act of 1862 and subsequent land grants, the great
continental railroad began to materialize. Even before Ben Holladay threw
in the towel, the rails were extending from east to west, toward Salt Lake
City. Ties were being laid along the dusty roadbed, and rails were being
spiked into place.

The stagelines were disappearing one by one. Before long, one of the
country's fondest memories would fade into oblivion. The magnificent
stagecoach, with its beautiful and feisty horses, was destined to become
another lost ripple in time.

On May 3, 1876, the last Barlow and Sanderson coach ran out of Pueblo.
Trinidad then became the northern terminus of the stageline to Santa Fe.
The Las Animas route continued to operate for some time. Two Barlow and
Sanderson stagelines in Colorado used the Mountain Branch of the Santa
Fe Trail and the Denver and Fort Union Road. Some lines continued long

after the railroad arrived; the line from Cucharas via the Sangre de Cristo Pass to Del Norte and from Cañon City up the Arkansas, through Poncha Pass to Saguache, and over Cochetopa Pass to the San Juan Country.

Barlow and Sanderson had coaches operating between West Las Animas and Trinidad during the summer of 1876. These coaches left Las Animas at 9 p.m. and, traveling through the night, reached Trinidad at 3 a.m. on the second morning so that they could connect with the Denver and Rio Grande train at El Moro.

Barlow and Sanderson also had the mail contract, so they picked up mail and passengers at El Moro and brought them into Trinidad. They used a four-mule stage and were called the "Southern Overland Mail Stage." This particular stagecoach had iron axles and heavy leather straps for springs. When the railroad came to Alamosa, the stageline shortened and only ran through Riverside and Venable to Del Norte and Lake City.

Some well-known drivers for Ben Holladay now operated between Del Norte and Jackson's—namely, L.M. Hill, James Billingsbee, Jim Madison, Jack Hayes, and a fellow from Kansas City, called "K.C. 'Big John' Stokes."

In 1877, Andy Woodruff and John Hock drove the stagecoach from Cañon City up the Arkansas River to Bale's Tavern. Several miles up the river was the settlement of South Arkansas, where coaches crossed the water and traveled on up to Poncha Pass, and then on to the San Luis Valley. In 1878, business picked up, and the post office department ordered Barlow and

This is a "photo op," as they say these days. A group of businessmen are seated on the last stage to leave Montrose and Ouray in August of 1887. The end of an impressive era!

Courtesy of Colorado Historical Society

*Competition from the railroads finally ended the stagecoach era. This is a
rare photo of both modes of transportation side-by-side.*
Courtesy of Western Reflections Publishing Company Photo Collection

Sanderson to increase their service to daily runs instead of tri-weekly ones
between South Arkansas and Del Norte, and Saguache and Lake City.

By 1880, the colorful stagecoach era had almost ended. Four-Mile
House would no longer hear the pounding of horses' hooves and the driver's shouts as they came into the station.

Some stagelines continued into the new century in small towns and settlements not yet reached by the railroads. For over fifty years, stagecoaches
traveled in the west and stayed one step ahead of the railroads. Needless to
say, the coming of railways caused the eventual disappearance of stagelines.
Stagecoaches enlivened the dusty streets of towns and cities, both large and
small. To an old pioneer, the stagelines were a happy memory.

It was often remarked by old timers that they would never forget the
brightly painted coaches and the teams of six splendid horses, guided
by the most expert of all the reinsman in the country. As they galloped
through the streets to the central station where they unloaded their passengers, mail, and express, they achieved the status of legend.

Oh! The old staging days! While we may be happy to have faster transportation these days, just writing about stagecoaches brings scenes to my
mind of beautiful coaches loaded for the West, hundreds of miles away.
Oh, how happy the passengers were when they first caught sight of the
magnificent Rocky Mountains! What a delight to see high mountain towns
surrounded by fields of wildflowers.

A BUMPY RIDE

The days were many when drivers of the stagecoaches had to bring the coach in when Indians were raiding; when outlaws had stolen all of the passengers' valuables, with perhaps injured or dead aboard; when coaches and horses covered with snow and ice eventually found their way home. No matter how many trials and tribulations the drivers faced, few, if any, ever deserted their post or failed to bring their precious cargo to safety. The many perils they encountered would try most men's souls, so surely no tribute of honor and praise is too great for the work they achieved back in the early days of Colorado.

CHAPTER FIFTEEN

COLORADO'S HISTORICAL
STAGECOACHES

Only a few authentic stagecoaches have survived over the years in Colorado. Some of Colorado's towns and cities have worked to maintain and restore them. Some of the stagecoaches found in museums around the state have actually been transplanted from other places; for example, one of the stagecoaches on display in western Colorado originally hailed from Iowa, and some others originally ran routes in California. Some coaches are made up of bits and pieces of many other coaches. When a stagecoach broke down and needed repair, often times, they used parts of another coach to repair it, especially in the later years. Then, in present times, some people have combined parts of stagecoaches to make a whole. One Colorado town, Mancos, has unique stagecoach reproductions worth mentioning.

The following is a listing of some of the stagecoaches that have been authenticated as actually being used in Colorado:

COLORADO SPRINGS

There are two examples of beautifully restored stagecoaches in the Ghost Town Museum and Park. The first coach, mostly gray and not completely restored, was a Wells Fargo and Company Express coach. This coach ran between Denver and Cheyenne in 1868, then to gold mining camps for the next forty years or so. It was pulled by four to six horses and carried eleven passengers, the driver, and the guard. "Coach" passengers sat on the roof or the outside rear seat. The middle jump seat held three people, their

Old authentic stagecoaches being restored at the Ghost Town Museum in Colorado Springs, Colorado. The sign says, "This historic coach first ran between Denver and Cheyenne in 1868, then to gold mining camps for the next 40 years."

Author's Photo Collection

backs leaning against a leather strap hung between the door pillars, leather curtains covering the windows. The second stage is a nicely restored coach called the "Sentinel Mountain Stage."

FAIRPLAY

South Park City has an authentic Abbot & Downing Mud Wagon built in Concord, New Hampshire. It was restored in 1990.

An Abbott & Downing mud wagon after restoration in 1990 at South Park City, Park County, Colorado.
Courtesy of South Park Historical Foundation

FT. GARLAND

Ft. Garland has an authentic Barlow and Sanderson Stagecoach in their museum. This coach provided basic transportation throughout the San Luis Valley of Colorado and New Mexico in the late 19th century. The stagecoach is a rare example of an Abbot-Downing mud wagon built about 1871.

An authentic Colorado stagecoach under protective cover at Ft. Garland, Colorado.
Author's Photo
Collection

A restored authentic Colorado stagecoach at the Otero County Museum in La Junta.

Courtesy of the Otero County Museum and Historical Society

LA JUNTA

The Otero Museum in La Junta has one of the rare authentic coaches found in Colorado. The coach is housed in the H.L. & Louise Boyd Coach House. This coach saw service between Atchison and Denver City until the railroad took over in 1876.

LONGMONT

On Highway 287, just one mile south of Longmont, is the Dougherty Museum. The Dougherty museum is open to the public and houses some beautiful specimens of years gone by, including a finely restored stagecoach that ran between Breckenridge and Fairplay. This coach sat for years at Tiny Town, where children climbed and played on it. Mr. Dougherty bought the old coach from the owner in Boulder and restored it.

MANCOS

Modern day Mancos has a unique business in its midst. Bartel's Stage Company is a reproduction of the old-time stagelines. It is an eerie, ghost-like reminder of the days of long ago. The one-hour or dinner tour travels down Weber Canyon to a beautiful old homestead, where you are treated to an authentic, old-west experience.

The Dougherty Museum in Longmont, Colorado, houses this finely restored stagecoach, which sat neglected at Tiny Town for many years.

Photo by Steven M. Burke

Bartel's Stage Company in Mancos, Colorado, is a unique business which gives its customers a glimpse into the past. If you like Colorado history, this may be the ride for you.

Author's Photo Collection

On display under a roof at the Montrose Historical Society Museum is this beautifully restored stagecoach. It was a Circle Route stage and ran from Montrose to Ouray, Silverton, and Durango for several years in the 1880s. No longer used in parades, it is cared for lovingly by Society members.

Author's Photo Collection

MONTROSE

Montrose is one of only a few fortunate towns to have a well-preserved and diligently restored Colorado stagecoach from the 1800s. This beautiful coach is of the mud wagon type that was often used in mountainous regions. The coach is housed under covers at the Montrose Historical Museum, and it is only brought out on rare occasions. It is extremely revered and cared for by Montrose Historical Musuem volunteers.

SILT

Long before Silt and New Castle, there was the town of Ferguson, named after Judge George Ferguson, who was the first settler in the valley. Besides a store and a post office on the Ferguson property, a ferry was built for crossing the Grand River (the Colorado River) to take supplies to New Castle settlers. The lovely old stagecoach ran from Rifle to Meeker and is now located in Silt.

STEAMBOAT SPRINGS

Steamboat Springs has two authentic stagecoaches on display. Both supposedly ran in that area during the 1800s.

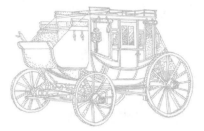

❧ THE STAGE COACH VOCABULARY ❧

BOOT: the leather baggage compartment at the rear of the stage and also under the driver's seat

BOX: the stagecoach driver's seat

BULL-WHACKER: a driver of a freight wagon, usually with oxen

CARRY-ALL: a light, covered carriage holding several people

CHARLIE: a stagecoach driver

CONCORD COACH: a stagecoach made by Abbott, Downing Company, Concord, New Hampshire

CORDUROY ROAD: a road created by logs laid across a swampy, low-lying area, placed together or "ribbed" like corduroy cloth

DRUMMER: a traveling salesman soliciting trade in the West after the Civil War

EXPRESSMAN: a messenger carrying express items

GROOM: a stableman who takes care of horses

HAME: one of two curved bars fitted to a horsecollar, holding the traces of a harness

HOSTLER: a stableman

JEHU: a name for a stagecoach driver, taken from the Biblical character who drove his vehicle fast and furiously

LEADERS: horses leading a four- or six-horse hitch

LINES: reins

REACHES: bars connecting rear axles with the forward part of the coach

A BUMPY RIDE

REINSMAN: a stagecoach driver

RIBBONS: reins

RIG: harness

ROAD AGENT: a stagecoach robber

"SHOTGUN": a stagecoach guard

SINGLETREE: horizontal crossbar, to the ends of which the traces of a harness are attached

STAGERS: men who ran the staging business

STAGING: the business of carrying people and mail by stagecoach

SWINGS: the horses in the middle position of a six-horse hitch

THOROUGHBRACE: a many-layered leather strap supporting the stage-coach body

TRACES: the side straps by which a horse pulls the stagecoach

WHEELERS: the horses nearest the front of the stagecoach

WHEELWRIGHT: a person who makes and repairs wheels

WHIPPLETREE: the horizontal bar at the front of the stagecoach, to which singletrees are attached

WHIP: a stagecoach driver

❧ ACKNOWLEDGMENTS AND SPECIAL THANKS ❧

I would like to thank the dozens of individuals and Colorado Historical Societies and Museums that responded to my call — from small towns to large cities all across the state. Without your valuable input and enthusiasm, this book would not have been possible.

Golden Pioneer Museum, Michelle Zupan, Curator

City of Greeley Museum, Peggy A. Ford, Archives and Research Coordinator

Fort Lupton Museum, N.D. Penfold, Curator

Fort Sedgwick Historical Society, Mary F. McKinstry, Archives Advisor

Limon Heritage Museum and Railroad Park, Vivian Lowe

Louisville Historical Museum, Carol Gleeson, Museum Coordinator

Rock Creek Farm Cultural Landscape District, (Historical Narrative)

Platteville, Colorado Historical Society, Sally Miller

Overland Trail Museum, Sterling, Colorado, Anna Mae Hagemeir, Curator

Yuma Museum, Inc., Shirley Starnes, Board Member

Longmont Museum, Erik Mason, Curator of Research and Information

Estes Park, (town of) Museum, Lisel Goetze Record, Museum Curator

Lyons Historical Society, Diane Goode Benedict

Lafayette Historical Society

Hotchkiss-Crawford Historical Society & Museum, Jacqueline Groll

San Luis Valley Historical Society

Chaffee County Historical Museum, Suzy Kelly

Cortez Cultural Center

Crested Butte Mountain Heritage Museum, Inc., Susan Medville, Director and Curator

Rio Grande County Museum and Cultural Center, Dr. A.J. Taylor, Cultural Director

Delta Historical Museum, Jim Wetzel, Museum Director
South Park City Historical Association.
La Plata County Historical Society, Marilyn Barnhart, Museum Volunteer
Ouray County Historical Society and Museum, Ann Connell Hoffman, Executive Director
San Juan Historical Society and Museum, Leroy Oldham, Treasurer
San Juan County Historical Society, Silverton, Beverly Rich, Chairman
Telluride Historical Museum, Shannon Clare Prewitt
Wilkinson Library, Telluride
Gilpin Historical Society, James J. Prochaska, P.E. Executive Director
Eagle Public Library, Jo Ann Steinfort, ECLD
South Park City, Carol Davis, Director, Curator
Historic Georgetown, Ann Izard, Office Manager
Grand Lake Area Historical Museum, Dave Lively & Corinne Lively
Kauffman House Museum
The Hayden Heritage Center, Jerry Green
Silt Historical Society, Alice Boulton, Alice Jones, and Bonnie Grant
Rio Blanco Historical Society, White River Museum, Meeker
Rangely Museum Society, Donald Peach
Redstone Historical Society, Ann Martin
Tread of the Pioneers Museum; Steamboat Springs, Candice Lombardo, Curator
Grand County Historical Society, Keith R. Nunn
Montrose County Historical Society and Museum, Marilyn Cox, Curator
Colorado Springs Pioneer Museum, Kelly Murphy, Research Archivist
Bent's Old Fort National Historic Site, U.S. Dept. of the Interior, Don Troyer
The Otero Museum Association, La Junta, Colorado, Don Lowman, President
The Huerfano Historical Society, Sue Duke, Board Member
Pioneer Historical Society, Las Animas, Barbara Busey, Secretary
Trinidad History Museum, Paula Manini, Curator
Ute Pass Historical Society and Pikes Peak Museum, Doris Breitenfeld, President
Westcliffe, Colorado, Historical Society, Linda Swift
Colorado State Library, Western Slope Division, Grand Junction
Montrose Regional Library
The Denver Public Library, Western History Dept. Phil Panum
Colorado Historical Society

ACKNOWLEDGMENTS AND SPECIAL THANKS

Carol Hunter, "Partnership for Access to the Woods," Hot Sulphur
    Springs
Hazel B. Petty, Alamosa
Marianne North, Casper, Wyo., Ramstetter History
Billy Walker, San Luis Valley Information, friend and neighbor
L.R. "Mac" McGraw, Gunnison Historical Museum, friend and fellow
    author
David Hughes, Old Colorado City
Richard Louden, Branson, Colorado, Santa Fe Trail Association
    Director
Ft. Collins Public Library, Rheba Massey, Local History librarian
Martha Boehner, Grand Lake, Colorado
Denver Public Library, Western History Collection, Ms. Coi Gehrig
Colorado Historical Society, Denver

Last, but not least, I would like to thank my daughter, Colleen Fraser,
and my granddaughter, Whitney J. Adams, for typing notes and using their
incredible organization skills.

My son, Steven M. Burke, Historical Architect with the General Services
Administration in Denver, Colorado, did the illustrations for this book.

If I have left anyone out, it was not intentional by any means. In any
case, all of the help given me was appreciated.

Marril Lee Burke

✒ BIBLIOGRAPHY ✒

Adams, Ramon, "Horses of the Stagelines," *Western Horseman Magazine*, 8/1950, Vol. XV, No. 8

Aldridge, Dorothy, *Historic Old Colorado City, Town of the Future*, Little London Press, 1996

Allen, Alonzo H., "Pioneer Life in Old Burlington, Forerunner of Longmont", *Colorado Magazine*

Armor, John B., *Colorado Magazine*, " Pioneer Experiences in Colorado, 1867

Austin, Hazel Baker, *Surface Creek County, Delta County Independent*, 1977

Baker, James H. and LeRoy R. Hafen, *History of Colorado:* "Staging, Packing and Freighting"

Banning, Captain William & George Hugh Banning, *Six Horses*, The Century Co., 1930

Bartz, James Lynn, *Company Property, Wells Fargo & CO's Express 1852-1918, The West Bound Stage*, 1993

Bates, Margaret, *Lake City, A Quick History*, Little London Press, 1973

Beardsley, Judge Arthur, *Transcription of Diaries of Judge Arthur Beardsley, The Glenwood Post*, Nov. 19, 1931

Benedict, Diane Goode, Lyons, *The Birth of a Quarry Town: 1880's*, Applications, Plus, 2002

Black, Robert C. III, *Island in the Rockies: The Pioneer Era of Grand County*, Grand County Pioneer Society, 1969

Blair, Edward, *Leadville: Colorado's Magic City*, Pruett Publishing Co., 1980

Bliss, Edward, *Colorado Magazine*, "Denver to Salt Lake by Overland Stage in 1862", Vol. 8, No. 5, 1931

Brotemarkle, Diane, *Old Fort St. Vrain*, Platteville Historical Society, 2001

Brown, Mabel E., "The Autobiography of Hester and Ann Brown", *Bits & Pieces, A Monthly Magazine of Western History*, 10/1969

Brown, Robert L., *An Empire of Silver*, Sundance Publications, Ltd., 1984

Burkey, Elmer R., *Colorado Magazine #9*, 1937, "The Georgetown-Leadville Stage,"

Buys, Christian J., *The Lost Journals of Charles S. Armstrong, 1867-1894*, Western Reflections Publishing Co., 2002

Colorado Historical Society, *Bent's Old Fort*, Colorado Historical Society, 1979

Colorado Miner, "Leadville in 1879", A Round Trip, 8/2/1879, Pg. 1, C. 3-7

BIBLIOGRAPHY

Conte, William R., *The Old Cripple Creek Stage Road*, Little London Press, 1984

Croffutt, George A., *Croffutt's Grip-Sack Guide to Colorado*, The Overland Publishing, Omaha, Nebraska, 1885

CWA Pioneer Interview: Doc. 347, Garfield County, "William Farnum", State Historical Society of Colorado, 1933/34

Darley, George M.D.D., *Pioneering in the San Juan's*, Fleming H. Revell Co., 1899

Dary, David, *The Santa Fe Trail, Its History, Legends, and Lore*, Penguin Group, 2000

Donaldson, Stanley, *Colorado Outdoors Magazine:* March/April 1964

Eichler, George R., *Colorado Place Names*, Johnson Publishing Co., 1977

Fanning, Clare, *Park County Echoes*

Fay, Abbott, *Beyond the Great Divide*, Western Reflections, 1999

Fossett, Frank, *Colorado: Its Gold and Silver Mines*, C.G. Crawford, Printer and Stationer, 1880

Fradkin, Philip L., *Stagecoach, Book One, Wells Fargo and the American West*, Simon and Schuster, 2002

Frazier, Jimmy Lee, "Early Stage Lines in Colorado", A Thesis, Denver University, 1959

Frederick, J. V., *Ben Holladay, The Stagecoach King*, University of Nebraska Press, 1940

Friggens, Myriam, *Tales, Trails and Tommyknockers*, Johnson Publishing Co., 1979

Ft. Collins Public Library, Local History Archive Contents, "Colorado Gold Rush, The Early Settlements and the Creation of Fort Collins, 1844-1866

Gilliland, Mary Ellen, *The Summit: A Gold Rush History Of Summit County*, Alpenrose Press, 1999

Glenwood Post, 12/19/1931; 8/17/1933

Greeley, Horace, *An Overland Journey from New York to San Francisco in the Summer of 1859*, University of Nebraska Press, 1860

Gregory, Doris, *History of Ouray, Vol. I*, Cascade Publishing Co., 1997

Hafen, Leroy R., *Colorado and Its People, Vol. I*, Lewis Historical Publishing, 1948

Hall, Frank, *History of Colorado, Vol. I*, Blakely Printing Co., 1889

Hall, Thomas B., M.D., *Medicine on the Santa Fe Trail*, Morningside Books 1971

Gilman, Musetta., *Pump on the Prairies; A Chronicle of a Road Ranch, 1859-1868*, Harlo Press, 1975

Herndon, Sarah Raymond, *The Diary of Sarah Raymond Herndon*, "Days on the Road: Crossing the Plains in 1865", Burr Printing House, 1902

Hill, Alice Polk, *Colorado Pioneers in Pictures and Story*, Brock-Hoffman Press, 1915

Hill, Alice Polk, *Tales of the Colorado Pioneers*, Brock-Hoffman Press, 1915

Houston, Grant, *Lake City Reflections*, B&B Printers, 1976

Hughes, David R., *Historic Old Colorado City*, Old Colorado City District, 1978

Jackson, W. Turrentine, *Wells Fargo in Colorado Territory*, A Monograph Series, #1, 1982, Colorado Historical Society.

Jessen, Ken, *Colorado Gunsmoke*, J.V. Publications, 1986

Johnson, Charles A., *Stagecoaches Along Cherry Creek*, Golden Bell Press, 1980

Jones, Elaine Hale, *Focus Magazine, Montrose Daily Press*, Winter Issue, 1979

Kelly, Suzy, *Buena Vista's Tales From the Past*, Wolf Graphic Arts, 2000

Kessler, Ron, *Retracing the Old Spanish Trail, North Branch,* Adobe Village Press, 1995

Kindquist, Cathy E., *Stony Pass: The Tumbling and Impetuous Trail,* San Juan Book Co., 1987

Lavender, David, *The Big Divide,* Castle Books, 2001

Leckenby, Charles, *Tread of the Pioneers,* Steamboat Springs Pilot, 1945

Lee, Mabel Barbee, *Cripple Creek Days,* University of Nebraska Press, 1958

Leigh, Kathy and Mary Saban, Website – "A Brief History of Stagecoaches", Created April 1, 2000, Copyright 2000-2004

Leonard, Sharron, *The Denver and South Park Stage Line,* No date or publisher

Long, Margaret, M.D., *Automobile Logs of the Smoky Hill Trail,* W. H. Kistler Stationery Co., 1943

McCullough, Frances, *The San Luis Valley Historian,* Vol. XXX, No. 3, 1998, "The Barlow and Sanderson Stage Line in the San Luis Valley"

Media, Cristo, *Trinidad History, 1997-2003, Colorado Prospector,* 1976

Mohisky, P.C., *Montrose Daily Press,* July 2, 1962

Monahan, Doris, *Destination: Denver City,* Swallow Press, 1985

Moody, Ralph, *Stagecoach West,* University of Nebraska Press, 1967

pbs.org/wildhorses/wh_man/wh_man3/html.

Peters, Bette D., *Denver's Four-Mile House,* Junior League of Denver, Inc. and the Golden Bell Press, 1980

Poet, S.E., *The Colorado Magazine,* Vol. IX, No. 1, "The Story of Tin Cup, Colorado," 1932

Probst, Nell Brown, *Forgotten People, A History of the South Platte Trail,* Pruett Publishing Co., 1979

Ramstetter, Charles and Mary, *John Gregory Country,* C Lazy Three Press, 1966

Ramstetter, James K., *Life in the Early Days,* Alameda Press, 1996

Rice, Frank, Unpublished Memoirs, "Stagecoaches", Courtesy of Doris Gregory

Riddle, Kenyon, *Records and Maps of the Old Santa Fe Trail,* Revised, Printed by Southwestern Printing Co., 1963

"The Roan Creek Toll Road, *Journal of the Western Slope,* Vol. 2, No. 1, Winter, Mesa College, 1987

Rockwell, Wilson, *Memoirs of a Lawman,* Sage Books, 1962

Rocky Mountain News, August 19, 1885, P.1, C. 5, Courtesy of DPL

Root, Frank A, and William Elsey Connelley, *The Overland Stage to California, Personal Reminiscences and Authentic History,* Published by Authors, 1901

Sammons, Loline, *They Came to Powderhorn,* Windell's Print Shop, 1981

Sanford, Albert B., *The Colorado Magazine,* "Mountain Staging in Colorado", Vol. IX, March 1932

Segale, Sister Blandina, *At the End of the Santa Fe Trail, Memoirs of Sister Blandina,* University of New Mexico Press, 1932

Settle, Mary and Raymond, *Empire on Wheels: Overland Routes to the Goldfields, 1859,* Personal Diaries, Stanford University Press, 1949

Shaw, Luella, *True History of Some of the Pioneers of Colorado,* 1909

"Silver Thread, Colorado", A Special Publication of Lake City *Silver World,* 1998

Shoemaker, Len, *Roaring Fork Valley,* Sage Books, 1958

Simmon, Virginia McConnell, *Bayou Salado, The Story of South Park,* Century One Press, 1966

BIBLIOGRAPHY

Simmons, Virginia McConnell, *The San Luis Valley: Land of the Six-Armed Cross,* Pruett Publishing Co., 1979

Simonin, Louis L., *The Rocky Mountain West in 1867,* "Transcontinental Stage," University of Nebraska Press, 1966

Sprague, Abner E., *My Pioneer Life: Memoirs of Abner E. Sprague,* Rocky Mountain Nature Assn., 1899

Spring, Agnes Wright, (Edited by), *The Diary of Mary Ellen Jackson Bailey,* City of Greeley Museum, 1869

Swisher, Sharon, "Ute Pass: A Concise History", *Teller County Divide Dispatch,* Commemorative Issue, 1992

Taylor, Bayard, *Colorado: A Summer Trip,* Edited by Wm. W. Savage, Jr., and James H. Lazalier, Delta Public Library, 1867

Taylor, Morris F., *First Mail West: Stagecoaching Lines On the Santa Fe Trail,* University of New Mexico Press, 1971

Taylor, Morris F., " Barlow and Sanderson Stage Lines in Colorado", *The Colorado Magazine,* No. 2, Spring, 1973

The Denver Field and Farm Magazine: 2/9/1907, Pg. 8; 7/27/1907, Pg. 8, No Author Given, "Frontier Sketches"

The Olden Days, World Press, 1954

The Rocky Mountain News: 2/22/1877, Pg. 4, C1; 9/1/1882, Pg. 2, C2; 7/12/1874, Pg. 4, CI; 4/30/1884, Pg. 4, C2

The San Luis Valley Historian, Vol. XXIV, No. 2, 1992, Chapter VIII, "The Wheels of Progress"

The Ute Chief, "Stage Accident" 8/13/1887 and "An Obituary" 9/24/1887

Time Life Books of the Old West – The Expressmen, St. Remy Press, 1974

Twain, Mark, *Roughing It,* American Publishing Co., 1872

Vandenbushe, Duane, *The Gunnison Country,* B&B Printers, 1980

Wallace, Betty, *Gunnison Country,* Sage Books, 1960

Warren, Harold, *Bits and Pieces of History Along the 285 Corridors,* K. R. Systems, 1994

Wheelock, Seymour E, *Colorado Heritage Magazine,* Colorado Historical Society, Issue 4, 1986

Wilcox, Patricia K., Editor, *76 Centennial Stories of Lakewood,* Lakewood Centennial-Bicentennial Commission, 1976

Wommack, Linda, *From the Grave,* Caxton Press, 1998

Wood, Frances and Dorothy, *I Hauled These Mountains In Here,* Caxton Printers, Ltd., 1977

Wootten, Richens, *Uncle Dick Wootten,* The Narrative Press, 2001

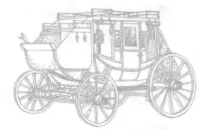

❧ INDEX ❧

INDEX

INDEX